Go Down, Moses

Go Down, Moses

A Celebration of the African-American Spiritual

RICHARD NEWMAN

Illustrations by Terrance Cummings

Foreword by Cornel West

Clarkson Potter/Publishers
New York

The musical notations accompanying selected spirituals were reproduced from *The Story of the Jubilee Singers; With Their Songs*, by J. B. T. Marsh, published in 1880 by The Riverside Press, Boston.

A Roundtable Press Book

Published by Clarkson N. Potter, Inc., 201 East 50th Street, New York, New York 10022. Member of the Crown Publishing Group.

Random House, Inc. New York, Toronto, London, Sydney, Auckland
http://www.randomhouse.com/

CLARKSON N. POTTER, POTTER, and colophon are trademarks of Clarkson N. Potter, Inc.

Printed in the United States of America

Design by Maggie Hinders

Library of Congress Cataloging-in-Publication Data
Newman, Richard
Go down, Moses: a celebration of the African-American spiritual.
Richard Newman. — 1st ed.
Includes bibliographical references.
1. Spirituals (Songs)—Texts. 2. African-Americans—Music. I. Title.
ML54.6.N495G6   1998
782.25'30268—dc21   97-23934

ISBN 0-609-60031-1

10 9 8 7 6 5 4 3 2 1

First Edition

For

Belynda Bady

"I hold my sister with a trembling hand,
I would not let her go!"

—from "Wrestling Jacob"

Contents

Acknowledgments

I WANT TO THANK EVERYONE WHO WAS HELPFUL AND ENCOURAGING during the pleasurable task of preparing this book. Marsha Melnick of Roundtable Press made the project happen, and Terrance Cummings's preliminary sketches made me want to create a manuscript worthy of his art. Allen Austin and Daphne Brooks gave me rare information; John Gennari and Guthrie Ramsey were models of scholarship; and Winthrop Ames Burr and Irene Monroe were supportive. Elleni Amlak and Cornel West gave their special friendship, and Saleema and Caswell Curtis provided a happy place to work over Thanksgiving vacation. I am always indebted to Henry Louis Gates, Jr., for inviting me to join the staff of the W. E. B. Du Bois Institute for Afro-American Research at Harvard University.

In working on the text, I thought often of my grandmother Glennie C. Burton (1875–1956) who first taught me the old gospel songs. During the preparation of the manuscript, William P. French died. His phenomenal knowledge of African-American books and bibliography was unsurpassed, and I am only one of many whose work was facilitated by his genius and who will miss his friendship as well as his erudition. Marguerite Harrison and Pamela Petro read this book's introductory essay and suggested improvements, as did James Danky (in a Cajun restaurant in Baton Rouge, Louisiana). The Northeast Seminar on Black Religion, meeting at Union Theological Seminary in New York on February 22, 1997, heard an earlier version of the introduction, entitled "The Irony of African-American Spirituals."

And there is always Belynda Bady.

RICHARD NEWMAN
Boston, Massachusetts

Foreword

THE AFRICAN-AMERICAN SPIRITUAL IS THE UNIQUE CULTURAL CREATION of New World modernity. As the distinguished historian Richard Newman (my friend and brother) rightly notes, the spirituals of American slaves of African descent constitute the first expression of American modern music. How ironic that a people on the dark side of modernity—dishonored, devalued, and dehumanized by the practices of modern Europeans and Americans—created the fundamental music of American modernity. Yet we still wonder and wrestle with what it is that makes these songs so *modern*—so powerful and poignant, so upsetting and unsettling, so soothing and comforting—to us late moderns.

As I grow older, I find it more and more difficult to read the heart-piercing lyrics of the spirituals. They not only invoke precious memories of beloved family and friends in those soul-stirring moments of my black church life; these songs also remind me of how difficult it is to engage in a deep-sea diving of the soul—a diving that may yield, if one is strong enough, blood-shot eyes and a tear-stained hope. When the slaves sang "Go Down, Moses," they put forward a political message of freedom and a hope for endurance in the face of death and despair *after* one arrives in the penultimate promised land of these United States. In short, the spirituals challenge any Enlightenment notion of human autonomy. They force us to confront the paradox of human freedom: we must be strong enough to resist the prevailing forms of bondage yet honest enough to acknowledge our weaknesses in the face of death and disappointment. This honesty about our weakness is itself a supreme form of strength that precludes paralysis and impotence.

Even more than the incredible blues and jazz of black people, the spirituals enact the initial "soul-making" of New World Africans. I deliberately use the Keatsian term here because the spirituals embody the creativity of courageous human beings who engaged the world of pain and trouble with faith, hope, spirit—and a kind of existential freedom even in slavery. The great W. E. B. Du Bois was the first public intellectual to grasp the significance of this complex "soul-making" of a people. In the last chapter of his classic *The Souls of*

Black Folk (1903), Du Bois probed the character of "the sorrow songs." He found a depth of articulate anguish unbeknownst in early American history. He also discovered a level of questioning about the nature of suffering that was alien to American culture. Du Bois was on the right track. The spirituals not only reveal the underside of America—in all of its stark nakedness; they also disclose the night side of the human condition—in all of its terror and horror. But they do so through an unequivocal Christian lens. So we often leap to the religious consolation of the spirituals without lingering for long on sadness and melancholia.

The African-American spirituals constitute the most sustained phenomenology of New World evil. In stark contrast to most artists and intellectuals of European descent, the illiterate, articulate slaves were obsessed with the problem of evil as it pertained to the most undeniable darkness of America—slavery. And though their resources were primarily religious, their existential insights go far beyond Christian dogma and doctrine.

Like Shakespeare's *Hamlet*, the spirituals are preoccupied with the memory of those beloved ones who have died and the desire for revenge against those who prosper from their evil doings. The major themes consist of mourning, suffering, resisting. Yet unlike Hamlet, who after much soul-searching commits murder, the heroes of the spirituals—namely, Jesus, Daniel, and Moses—triumph because they find great strength in an all-embracing love and mercy.

The spirituals have perplexed critics primarily because of this uncanny tension between a profound pagan sense of the tragic and a deep Christian sense of justice. Ironically, both understandings assume the intractability of white supremacy in American life—be it slavery, Jim Crow, or postmodern cultural putdown—and view the preservation of the human soul under such dishonored conditions as the major challenge. Emerson was concerned with developing the human character through self-reliance within an American context of numbing conformity; the spirituals, on the other hand, focus on forging human integrity through self-respect within an American context of white hatred and fear of black folk.

I find it useful to compare the spirituals—the grand lyrical expressions at the initial moments of American self-definition—with the great lyrical poets of marginalized European peoples. In fact, two of the greatest lyrical poets of modern Europe—Fyodor Tyutchev of Russia and Giacomo Leopardi of Italy—have fascinating elective affinities with the spirituals. Both are rooted in Christian soils—Russian Orthodoxy and Roman Catholicism—yet sprout their poetic wings far above it. Both are distrustful of European arrogance and Enlightenment illusions and are obsessed with the night side of Western civilization. In regard to form, both deploy a kind of rhythmic repetition that plays with linguistic pacing, revealing an obsession with human time. This obsession often yields a privileging of silence by means of poetry, a call for music and song that goes beyond mere language.

The slaves' own self-conscious grasp of their inability to capture in language the depths of "Deep River" resonates with the spirit of Tyutchev's classic "Silentium!" (1829).

> *Speak not, lie deep, do not reveal*
> *Things that you wish or things you feel;*
> *Within your soul's protected mine*
> *Let them ascend and then decline*
> *Like silent stars in heaven bleak;*
> *Admire their sheen—but do not speak.*
>
> *How can a heart be put in words?*
> *By others—how can one be heard?*
> *Will people know what you live by?*
> *A thought expressed becomes a lie.*
> *Don't muddy springs that are unique:*
> *Drink from their depth—but do not speak.*
>
> *Live only in yourself encased;*
> *Your soul contains a world of chaste,*
> *Mysterious thoughts, which outside noise*
> *Robs of their magic and destroys;*
> *The rays of morning make them weak—*
> *Enjoy their song but do not speak! . . .*

Tyutchev's animation of nature and celebration of the landscape seem to suggest a latent pantheism alien to the spirituals. But Tyutchev neither worships nature nor equates God with it. Like the spirituals, he uses the majesty of God manifest in nature to highlight the misery of humankind. Like his friend and intellectual mentor, Freidrich Schelling, all forms of idealism, romanticism, or pantheism run headlong into the bedrock, the recalcitrant reality, of evil. Tyutchev's poetry wrestles with the dark questions of Schelling's classic work on theodicy, *On the Essence of Human Freedom* (1809): Does the seeming ineradicability of the nonrational signify the triumph of the absurd? Does the apparent intractability of the unfathomable point to the victory of evil? Are there countervailing forces—divine and human—that offset and overcome "the veil of sadness which is spread over all nature, the deep, unappeasable melancholy of all life"?

These foundation-shaking queries rendered Schelling silent for over forty years, pushed some slaves to sing sorrow songs, and drove Tyutchev to write in "Our Age" (1851):

> *Not flesh but spirit is depraved today,*
> *And Man feels miserable and tormented . . .*
> *He hates his darkness, tries to break away,*
> *But, once in daylight, riots discontented.*
>
> *The unendurable he must endure,*
> *From lack of faith as in a desert burning . . .*
> *He perishes . . . but, weak and insecure,*
> *He will not pray for faith, despite his yearning.*
>
> *He will pronounce, repenting, nevermore*
> *The words, "O Everlasting One! I ask you,*
> *For I believe in Thee, unlock this door*
> *And, in my disbelief, come to my rescue! . . ."*

If Fyodor Tyutchev represents a useful comparison to the religious nature of the spirituals, then Giacomo Leopardi may yield insights into the tragic nature of the spirituals. Haunted by a sense of his own ugliness (he was a disfigured hunchback) and overwhelmed by unrequited love, Leopardi's poetry—like the spirituals—soars to the sky on the wings of incredible grief and unbearable sorrow. He begins his famous "Night Song of a Nomadic Shepherd in Asha" (1830):

> *Moon, moon of silence, what are you doing,*
> *Tell me what you're doing in the sky?*

Later in the poem he writes:

> *A man comes struggling into the world;*
> *His birth is in the shadow of death;*
> *Pain and suffering*
> *Are his first discoveries;*
> *And from that point*
> *His mother and father try*
> *To console him for having been born.*

Leopardi ends the poem with echoes of Sophocles, Job, and the slave author of "Am I Born to Die?"

> *Perhaps if I had wings to soar*
> *Over the clouds and count the stars,*
> *Or run like thunder from peak to peak,*
> *I'd be happier, my gentle flock,*
> *I would be happier, radiant moon.*
> *Or maybe I simply miss the truth*
> *In thinking of other lives like this:*
> *Perhaps whatever form it takes*
> *Or wherever it comes to pass—*
> *Lair of beast or baby's cradle—*
> *To that creature being born*
> *Its birth day is a day to mourn.*

Similar to the slave author's lament, "Lord, I wish I had never been born," Leopardi pursues this tragic theme in "Sappho's Last Song" (1822):

What offence, what loathsome crime marked me
Before I was born, making Heaven and the fall
Of Fortune frown as they did? What sin
Did I commit as a child—when one can know
No wrong at all—that my iron-dark thread of life,
Lacking all the summer colors of youth,
Lay twisted on Fate's implacable spindle? Reckless
Words fly from your mouth: A hidden purpose
Fashions whatever has to happen. Everything is hidden
Except our pain. We come, a forsaken race,
Crying into the world, and the gods
Keep their own counsel . . .

Leopardi's pagan humanism departs from the Christian sense of providence found in the spirituals. Yet the passionate questioning and desperate seeking of the spirituals reveal, at times, an anger with God. For Leopardi, this anger fueled by unjustified grief yields a spiritual humility in a godless universe, an eternal silence in an infinite space. In "Dream" (1828), he cries:

And random suffering cancels all
Such raw, unripened knowledge.—Hush,
I said, my poor dear, hush . . .

. . . But alas, what is
This thing called death? It seems, if ever,
I should be able this day to say for sure, and so
Guard this helpless self against heartless stars.

For the spirituals, this anger fanned by unmerited misery offers a spiritual humility in a Christian world, an uncanny spirit of combat on a treacherous terrain ruled by a majestic yet mysterious God of love and mercy. Just as the epigraph of Leopardi's masterpiece, "Broom or the Flower of the Desert" (1836), is John 3:19, "And men loved darkness rather than light" so the epigraph of one the greatest spirituals, "Didn't My Lord Deliver Daniel," could be John 3:16, "God so loved the world that He sent His only begotten son . . ." The spirituals knew that men loved darkness yet they held out for a light of deliverance in a vanquishing and vanishing world. Says Leopardi in "Broom":

> *Nothing but ruins now left*
> *Where this sweet flower takes root*
> *And, it seems, takes pity*
> *On the suffering of others, filling*
> *The air with fragrance, a touch*
> *Of consolation in the wasteland . . .*

For the slaves, God's revelation in Christ is the sole flickering candle against the darkness of American slavery and human finitude. Their social "blackness" (shame) and existential "emptiness" (anxiety) find help only in divine deliverance (Christ). For Leopardi, only empathy and social solidarity can push back the darkness of oppression and death, yet even heroic efforts may be "built on sand." Speaking to both deserted persons and desert flowers, Leopardi concludes his greatest poem:

> *'Til that time comes you won't bow down*
> *Like cowards before the one who'll destroy you,*
> *Seeking your salutation in vain; and you won't*
> *Raise vainglorious heads to the stars*
> *Or up above this wasteland where*
> *By chance and not by choice you have*
> *Your birthplace and your home; and still*
> *You're wiser and that much less weak*
> *Than man, inasmuch as you don't believe*
> *These delicate stems of yours have been,*
> *By yourself or the fatal scheme*
> *Of things, fashioned for immortality.*

The greatest spiritual, "Nobody Knows the Trouble I See, Lord," speaks to dishonored persons whose humanity had been rendered invisible by physical chains and psychic blinders. As in Leopardi, this human condition is one of darkness. The spiritual explicity asks for prayer—for empathy and social solidarity—"to drive old Satan away." This kind of support, one that constitutes a loving tradition of resistance, yields a joy and even ecstasy because it is undergirded by a Lord who is able to deliver Daniel. "Glory Hallelujah!" Yet prayer for the slaves was much like the songs themselves—an artistic expression that gives form to the cry for help in the midst of great trials and tribulations. Prayers, poetry, spirituals—all are passionate acts of will that honestly express the human need for help and support. The towering literary artist of our own blood-drenched century, Franz Kafka notes:

> *Art like prayer is a hand outstretched in the darkness,*
> *seeking for some touch of grace which will transform*
> *it into a hand that bestows gifts.*

Is it mere accident that "A Love Supreme" (1964)—the masterpiece of the greatest musical artist of our time and the grand exemplar of twentieth-century black spirituality, John Coltrane—is cast in the form of prayer? The slave authors of the spirituals, Fyodor Tyutchev, Giacomo Leopardi, Franz Kafka, and John Coltrane all engaged in a Keatsian "soul-making" in that they courageously confronted the darkness in and of modernity with artistic integrity and genuine spirituality. They did so with, in the words of William James:

> *Not the conception or the intellectual perception of evil,*
> *but the grisly blood-freezing heart-palsying sensation of it close*
> *upon one . . . How irrelevantly remote seem all our usual refined*
> *optimisms and intellectual and moral consolations in presence*
> *of a need of help like this! Here is the real core of the religious*
> *problem: Help! Help!*

The African-American spiritual—with its motifs of homelessness, name-lessness, and hope against hope—is the first modern artistic expression of this human outcry in the New World.

CORNEL WEST
Harvard University

Introduction

OVER THE YEARS IMMIGRANT GROUPS FROM ACROSS THE WORLD HAVE brought their national music to America, but aside from Native Americans, African Americans were the first to create an indigenous American music. The African experience was unique: stolen from their homes, transported involuntarily in chains, and sentenced to lifetimes of slavery, Africans were cut off from their various ethnic cultures, including their languages. Their first challenge in America, therefore, was to transcend their different traditions and come together as a single people. During that process, an astonishing and still little recognized cultural interchange and transformation took place.

As Africans were themselves uniting, they were at the same time thrown into constant contact with Europeans. The first Africans were brought to British North America at Jamestown, Virginia, in early August 1619. Before the Pilgrims landed at Plymouth Rock, then, the cultures of the two continents and the two races had begun the process of interaction and synthesis. It was a long time before white Americans believed that black Americans even had a history, let alone that it was so intertwined with their own that African-American history is actually American history. Now, however, as we come to understand just how combined and intermingled African and European cultures really were, we can see that American history is actually African-American history as well.

This melding is the basis and background for the emergence of the spirituals as a new and distinct musical form. As Benjamin Mays, the longtime president of Morehouse College, explained, "The creation of the spirituals was no accident. It was a creation born of necessity, so that the slave might more adequately adjust himself to the conditions of the new world."

Music and dance were vital dimensions of daily African life, and if slaves could not carry physical cultural artifacts with them to North America, they could, and did, bring their extensive and complex expressive cultures. It has been suggested that the earliest synthesis of Europe and Africa, and the first manifestation of African-American culture, took place on the slave ships during the horrendous Middle Passage between Africa and America. On the upper decks, slaves were forced under the lash to dance for exercise. Whatever the rhythms, patterns, music, and lyrics consisted of, they have been lost, but it was here that Africa and Europe met, that the process of creative interaction began, and that a vital new people and culture suffered the pains of birth.

The emergence of the spirituals is rooted in the encounter between African traditional life and the evangelical Protestant Christianity of the white American South. In that encounter the African village became the slave quarters and the slave congregation; the root doctor and griot, or storyteller, became the preacher-healer-song leader; spirit possession became the ecstasy of emotional revivalism; the circle dance became the ring shout; community participation became call-and-response; and the history of the ancestors became the narratives of the King James Bible. The theologian James Cone writes: "Through song they built new structures for existence in an alien land. The spirituals enabled blacks to retain a measure of African identity while living in the midst of American slavery, providing both the substance and the rhythm to cope with human servitude."

Today, according to the Library of Congress, we know of more than six thousand spirituals, although some exist only in fragments. Many spirituals have been lost forever—especially, we can assume, the earliest ones, as well as earlier versions of spirituals that have survived. The creation of the spirituals was organic, coming up from below, coming up from the people. It was a living folk art—with no authors, no composers, no dates, no lyricists, nothing written down, no fixed or authoritative texts—belonging to the community. The same phrases might appear in different songs, the same words might be sung to different tunes, and every set of lyrics had its variants across the plantation South.

Like the blues and jazz, for which they are the foundation, spirituals are improvisational. Usually a lead singer, although it could be anyone, would sing one line, and the others present would repeat it or reply with a familiar chorus in a call-and-response antiphony. Anyone could add new verses, and the best of these survived through a kind of natural selection. In singing the spirituals there was no separation between artist and audience, no distinction between creator and performer, a style that continued in later African-American music. "The singer is found by the song," the writer James Baldwin once commented. Spirituals were never meant to be performed on a concert stage. As folklorist Zora Neale Hurston points out, these songs are authentic only when they are sung by and for the people themselves, expressing their feelings of the moment and of the situation. They are spontaneous songs, Hurston says, whose "truth dies under training like flowers under hot water."

With some exceptions, African-American slaves were a nonliterate people with a strong and sophisticated oral tradition of songs, stories, historical accounts, proverbs, and tales. Facility with speech, cleverness with words, verbal wit, and dramatic oratory were—and remain—highly admired qualities within the African-American community. The spirituals are poems, expressing emotions, full of symbols, tropes, and metaphors, and often containing layers of meaning. Their use of vernacular language is sometimes striking. Deceptively simple, spirituals can rise to piercing directness and immediacy. Many have lines of poetic power and a provocative turn of phrase:

> *I sweep my house with the gospel broom*
> *I'm a-rolling in Jesus' arms*
> *I'm going to sit down at the welcome table*
> *Fix me, Jesus, fix me right*
> *If anybody asks you what's the matter with me / Just tell him I say /*
>   *I'm running for my life*
> *Mary set her table / 'Spite of all her foes*

Sometimes entire lyrics are startlingly innovative in their use of words:

> *When the preacher, the preacher done give me over,*
> *King Jesus is my only friend.*
> *When my house, my house become a public hall,*
> *King Jesus is my only friend.*
> *When my face, my face become a looking glass,*
> *King Jesus is my only friend.*

The spirituals are essentially religious songs. Early white American Protestants sang the psalms in meter along with the traditional stately hymns of the church. But on the rural frontier, religion was more informal, more individualistic and personal, more emotional, and a new kind of vernacular music emerged to reflect the new religious democracy. Called "spiritual songs," they were religious in nature but lacked the dignity of conventional hymns. The African-American slave songs influenced spiritual songs, so it is not surprising that the name spirituals was given to these religious slave songs when, following the Civil War, they were first recognized as a discrete African-American creation.

The earliest known mention of a distinctive black religious music, according to scholar Dena J. Epstein, was published in 1819 by John F. Watson, a white man who was criticizing black "excesses" at Methodist camp meeting revivals. His words are revealing:

> We have, too, a growing evil in the practice of singing in our places
> of public and societal worship, merry airs, adapted from old songs,
> to hymns . . . most frequently composed and first sung by the illit-
> erate blacks of the society. . . . [At camp meetings] in the blacks'
> quarter, the colored people get together, and sing for hours
> together, short scraps of disjointed affirmations, pledges, or
> prayers, lengthened out with long repetitive choruses. These are all
> sung in the merry-chorus manner of the southern harvest field, or
> husking frolic method of the slave blacks; and also very like the
> Indian dances. With every word so sung, they have a sinking on
> one or other leg of the body alternately, producing an audible
> sound of the feet at every step and as manifest as the steps of actual
> Negro dancing in Virginia, etc. If some in the meantime sit, they
> strike the sounds alternately on each thigh.

Despite his critical stance, Watson's description is full of relevant and important information. African Americans may have been segregated at camp meetings but they were present and participating. We can see the process of cultural interaction and blending taking place: as Watson's words "first sung by" suggest, whites picked up both songs and styles from blacks. Whatever the meldings, however, spirituals remained distinctly different from white spiritual songs, and the African retentions and influences are clear: the "long repetitive choruses," the "merry airs," and, most clearly, the elements of African dance in the rhythmic body movements.

Watson's comparison to harvest and husking songs shows the relationship of spirituals to other slave musical creations such as work songs, love songs, shouts, songs for dancing, and railroad songs. And the reference to "actual Negro dancing" reveals that black dance, with its strong African character, was perceived as distinct from European forms of dance. In a fascinating aside, Watson even touches on the possibility of Native American influences. Overall, Watson's account tells us that spirituals were well formed by 1819. Of course, we do not know what the black community sang by and for itself when it was not in the presence of whites, but we can assume it was less, rather than more, European.

What was the content of these slave songs? "The clue to the meaning of the spirituals," writes the theologian Howard Thurman, "is to be found in religious experience and spiritual discernment." As religious songs, the spirituals reflect many of the characteristics of the evangelical Protestantism of the day: the centrality of the Bible, the sovereignty of a God of justice, personal accountability for one's life on earth, trust in Jesus, and hope for eternal life in Heaven. Spirituality accompanied theology, and the spirituals reveal the slaves' deep personal and collective faith. Tied to this was a surprisingly hopeful optimism, which transcended the wretchedness of the slave experience. The anguished cry of despair in one version of "Nobody Knows the Trouble I See" ends with an affirmation as positive as it is unexpected:

> *Nobody knows the trouble I see,*
> *Nobody knows my sorrow.*
> *Nobody knows the trouble I see.*
> *Glory, Hallelujah!*

Some slave owners permitted white ministers and missionaries to preach to their slaves. The ministers' usual text was Colossians 3:22, "Servants, obey in all things your masters." But as they accepted the Protestant principle of scriptural authority, African Americans would hear or read the rest of the Bible, and they would encounter there another message altogether. In the words of James Cone, they discovered that "faith, as trust in God's Word of liberation, stands at the heart of biblical revelation" and that "God's liberation is at work in the world."

The biblical narrative that resonated most strongly with the slaves' bitter experiences, while at the same time promising hope for deliverance, was the story of the Israelites' bondage in Egypt. Moses is one of the most often mentioned persons in the spirituals. African Americans also identified with Noah, Daniel, Jonah, and others of God's faithful people who were rescued by a just God from a sinful world of unfaithfulness and oppression. The nonliterate slaves told the biblical stories by turning them into songs, which, when stitched together, recount the Scriptures from beginning to end—from Adam in the garden to John the revelator. The Bible is whole: personalities from both Testaments are indiscriminately lumped together. Jesus appears in several images: the innocent child, the victim of whipping, the king on a milk-white horse who protects his subjects. In James Cone's potent words, Jesus is even "God's black slave who has come to put an end to human bondage."

"Go Down, Moses" is perhaps the best-known spiritual. The direct and powerful appeal for human liberation exemplifies the theme and thread of freedom that runs through all spirituals. It has even been attributed to Nat Turner, either as author or subject—the leader of a slave revolt in Southampton County, Virginia, in 1831, the bloodiest of the 250 North American slave revolts. The message of "Go Down, Moses" was so clear that some slaveholders forbade its singing on their plantations. Its great popularity and widespread use not only demonstrate the inspiration the slaves got from the Bible and their identification with the chosen Israelites, but show that freedom for the slaves was a physical reality in this world, and not merely an otherworldly aspiration.

The metaphorical nature of the spirituals has been greatly debated and disputed. Most white critics have thought that the spirituals were essentially concerned with life in heaven, undoubtedly because they believed black slaves were docile folks, content with their lives of servitude. But African Americans have always known that the spirituals are full of coded words and secret signals, messages between and among only themselves, communications that could be concealed from the white master class. The testimonies of Frederick Douglass and other self-liberated slaves who recounted their experiences confirm that the spirituals were full of symbolic language. The slaves themselves were God's people, Israel. Moses was a leader and deliverer. Egypt or Babylon represented the South, and hell the Deep South. Pharaoh was a slave owner. The River Jordan was the Ohio River or a similar body of water between the North and the South. The Red Sea was the Atlantic Ocean. Home, Canaan, camp meeting, or the Promised Land were Africa, the free states, Canada, or Liberia. Any agency of travel or movement—trains, shoes, chariots, wheels—spoke of escape.

This political aspect of the spirituals is perhaps their most important legacy, both historically and now; it cannot be overemphasized. A few lyrics are obvious: "Master going to sell us tomorrow" or "No more hundred lash for me / Many thousand gone." Numerous verses mention family members, remembering those sold away in slave owners' cruel disregard for human relationships. Other songs are more subtle. Frederick Douglass said that the words "Run to Jesus / Shun the danger" first gave him the idea of escaping from bondage. Other songs are also about running away, the Underground Railroad, and God's promised destruction of a sinful social order: "I don't intend to die in Egypt land"; "When the train comes along / I'll meet you at the station"; "God's going to set the world on fire." There are songs of the liberation that is to come: "You can hinder me here, but you can't hinder me there" are lines from "Free at Last," the spiritual Martin Luther King, Jr., recited in his 1963 March on Washington speech, "I Have a Dream." There is a profoundly radical, even revolutionary, thrust to these songs, as the slaves expanded their struggle for freedom to encompass all the disinherited: "Didn't my Lord deliver Daniel / And why not every man?"

The anonymous slave poets, those "black and unknown bards," as the poet James Weldon Johnson called them, were the progenitors of a great new Afro-poetics. The first African American to publish a book was Phillis Wheatley, a slave whose book of poetry was published in London in 1773. Despite her unappreciated references to Africa and liberty, she nonetheless followed the

European and classical literary tradition. It is the vibrant vernacular language of the spirituals, their marriage of Africa and Europe, and their grand obsession with freedom that makes them unique. Antonín Dvořák, the Czech composer, recognized this early on and incorporated African-American themes into his *New World Symphony* of 1893. He writes, "The so-called plantation songs are among the most striking and appealing melodies that have been found this side of the water."

African-American spirituals have not been particularly well documented, either historically or musically. African music, especially its complex polyrhythms, is not easily comprehended by Western-trained ears, and whites of the slavocracy did not take the slaves' music seriously or treat it with respect. There are surprisingly few references to spiritual in antebellum diaries and letters. The first sympathetic interest on the part of whites came during the Civil War from abolitionists in and out of the U.S. Army who heard the singing of "contrabands," self-liberated slaves who had escaped to the protection of Union lines.

One of the earliest reports came from the Reverend Lewis Lockwood, a white agent of the American Missionary Association sent to do educational and relief work among contrabands at Fortress Monroe on Chesapeake Bay. Lockwood first heard black singing on September 3, 1861, and soon provided the *New York Tribune* with the text of "Go Down, Moses," its first appearance in print. The discussion over the accurate representation of both African-American words and music began then and has not yet been resolved. Curiously, little attention has been paid to the use of spirituals in the writing of African Americans. Martin Delany's novel *Blake, or The Huts of America*, issued serially in 1881 and 1882, includes what the scholar Allen Austin calls "the largest compendium of black-created or black-adapted verses and songs in the antebellum period." Pauline E. Hopkins also utilizes spirituals significantly in her novel *Of One Blood, or The Hidden Self*, serialized in the *Colored American Magazine* in 1902 and 1903.

One achievement of the spirituals was to offer the nation its first authentic African-American music and lyrics. White America had been so fascinated with black life that throughout the nineteenth century the country's most popular entertainment was minstrel shows. Minstrelsy was a grotesque white parody of black singing, dancing, humor, and style, even though it was based, as blues composer W. C. Handy and others have pointed out, on real African-American expressive culture. In addition to minstrelsy's racist stereotypes, there was a less demeaning form of white imitation in the sentimental ballads of Stephen Foster. Foster had heard black songs and adapted them for white audiences, combining theft with homogenization—a practice that continued with ragtime and jazz.

Despite the fact that the spirituals were, in the scholar W. E. B. Du Bois's words, "the slaves' one articulate message to the world," the truth is that they were nearly lost. Beyond the flutter of abolitionist interest during the Civil War, there were few white people who had heard spirituals, and the freedpeople were eager to forget them as a relic of the slavery they were trying to put behind them. In particular, the small but influential African-American middle class was anxious to embrace European culture in order to prove that they were as capable and deserving as white people. A similar attitude can be seen later in relation to blues, jazz, rap, Ebonics—all expressions that have bubbled up from the underclass to challenge and even subvert the dominant cultural establishment.

The spirituals were actually saved for posterity by a small group of African-American men and women at Fisk University, a school for freedpeople established just after the Civil War in Nashville, Tennessee, by the American Missionary Association. The school was so overcrowded and so poor that students and faculty sold the iron from Nashville's former slave pens to buy spelling books. George White, Fisk's music teacher, organized a small choir he called the Jubilee Singers, and then hit upon the idea of taking them on a concert tour to raise money for the floundering college. Leaving Nashville in 1871 on borrowed money, the choir was markedly unsuccessful until they began singing spirituals to white church groups in the North, who were former abolitionists sympathetic to African Americans, their struggle for freedom, and their culture. Suddenly the Singers became a smashing success—they sang in Henry Ward Beecher's Brooklyn church, for President Ulysses Grant, and for Queen Victoria in England. (At the request of the British Prime Minister's wife, the Fisk Jubilee Singers sang "John Brown's Body" for the Grand Duchess Maria Fyodorovna, whose father-in-law, Czar Alexander II, had just liberated the Russian serfs.) The Fisk Jubilee Singers rescued the spirituals and made it respectable to sing them. As the music scholar Mary Jo Sanna points out, "Negro spirituals" became commonplace in American popular culture, "the only way whites knowingly and willingly participated in the contributions of blacks to American culture."

The lasting power of the spirituals lies in their message. Calling the spirituals "sorrow songs," W. E. B. Du Bois wrote, "They are the music of an unhappy people, of the children of disappointment; they tell of death and suffering and unvoiced longing toward a truer world." There is a little-noted parallel between the spirituals and their secular offspring, the blues, songs that also deal with the sadness and melancholy of men and women struggling with the "blue devils" of despair. The contemporary writer Ralph Ellison describes the redemptive function of blues: "The blues is an impulse to keep the painful details and episodes of a brutal experience alive in one's aching consciousness, to finger its jagged edge, and to transcend it, not by the consolation of philosophy, but by squeezing from it a near-tragic, near-comic lyricism." The same holds true for the spirituals. These songs reflect the slaves' sorrows, but the pain is transformed by the act of expression, by fingering the "jagged edge." They are metamorphosed, like the blues, into songs of resilience and overcoming, and even into affirmations of divine redemption and human triumph.

Songs of
faith

Deep River

THE AFRICAN-AMERICAN THEOLOGIAN HOWARD THURMAN FOUND
*"Deep River," with its image of life as a river, to be the most universal of all the
spirituals. And the white literary critic H. L. Mencken said the unknown slave
author of "Deep River" "was one of the greatest poets we have ever produced." The
"campground" in the song refers to both Heaven and the free land of the North. One
ex-slave told a Quaker abolitionist that for many slaves the image meant returning
to Africa.*

want to cross o - ver in - to camp ground.

1. Oh, don't you want to go   to that Gos - pel-feast, That
2. I'll go in - to hea-ven,   and take my seat,
3. Oh, when I get to heav'n, I'll walk all a -bout. There's

1. pro - mis'd land where all   is   peace? Lord,   I
2. Cast my crown at Je - sus' feet. Lord,   I
3. nobody there for   to turn me out. Lord,   I

want to cross o - ver in - to camp ground, Lord, I

want to cross o - ver in - to camp ground, Lord, I

want to cross o - ver in - to camp ground, Lord, I

want to cross o - ver in - to camp ground.

Adam's in the Garden Pinning Leaves

MAINTAINING THE AFRICAN TRADITION OF RECALLING AND RECITING *history through songs, the slaves turned biblical stories into spirituals. This one is from the creation account in the third chapter of Genesis. God seeks Adam in the Garden of Eden. Adam, however, is "laying low," making an apron of leaves to cover his newly discovered nakedness after eating the forbidden fruit.*

First time God called Adam,
Adam refused to answer,
Adam's in the garden laying low;
Second time God called Adam,
Adam refused to answer,
Adam's in the garden laying low.

Eve, where is Adam,
O, Eve, where is Adam?
O, Eve, where is Adam?
Lord, Adam's in the garden pinning leaves.

Next time God called Adam,
God hollered louder,
Adam's in the garden pinning leaves;
Next time God called Adam,
God hollered louder,
Adam's in the garden pinning leaves.

You, Eve, can't see Adam,
You, Eve, can't see Adam,
O, Eve, can't see Adam,
Lord, Adam's behind the fig tree pinning
    leaves.

Ain't Got Time to Die

IN ATTEMPTING TO UNDERSTAND THE SPIRITUALS, IT IS DIFFICULT TO
*pinpoint which elements are African, which come from North American evangelical
Protestant hymns, and which reflect the slaves' own creativity—primarily in melding the first two elements. We do know, however, that the Africanisms tend to lie at
the heart of the spirituals while the "outer covering" is European. The first line of
this song sounds like an evangelical hymn, but the four lines of repetition that follow show the pattern of African rhythm.*

Lord, I keep so busy praising my Jesus,
   Keep so busy praising my Jesus,
   Keep so busy praising my Jesus,
   Keep so busy praising my Jesus,
   Keep so busy praising my Jesus,
Ain't got time to die.

'Cause when I'm healing the sick,
   When I'm healing the sick,
   When I'm healing the sick,
   When I'm healing the sick,
   When I'm healing the sick,
Ain't got time to die.

'Cause it takes all of my time,
   It takes all of my time,
   It takes all of my time,
To praise my Jesus,
Ain't got time to die.

If I don't praise Him,
If I don't praise Him,
If I don't praise Him,
The rocks gonna cry out,
Glory and honor, glory and honor,
Ain't got time to die.

Lord, I keep so busy working for the
   Kingdom,
   Keep so busy working for the Kingdom,
   Keep so busy working for the Kingdom,
   Keep so busy working for the Kingdom,
Ain't got time to die.

'Cause when I'm feeding the poor,
   When I'm feeding the poor,
   When I'm feeding the poor,
I'm working for the Kingdom,
And I ain't got time to die.

Lord, I keep so busy serving my Master.
   Keep so busy serving my Master.
   Keep so busy serving my Master.
Ain't got time to die.

'Cause when I'm giving my all,
   When I'm giving my all,
   When I'm giving my all,
I'm serving my Master,
Ain't got time to die.

The Angels Done Bowed Down

BEFORE ANYTHING ELSE, THE SPIRITUALS ARE HYMNS OF PRAISE TO GOD. *But they are sung to a God of righteousness who will right the wrongs of a sinful slaveholding world. Jesus' crucifixion means not only that the very angels bowed down, but that in this life "the time that's been will be no more."*

O, the angels done bowed down,
O, the angels done bowed down,
O, the angels done bowed down,
O, yes, my Lord.

While Jesus was hanging upon the cross,
The angels kept quiet till God went off,
And the angels hung their harps on the
   willow trees,
To give satisfaction till God was pleased.

His soul went up on the pillar of cloud,
O, God He moved and the angels did bow,
Jehovah's sword was at His side,
On the empty air He began to ride.

"Go down angels to the flood,
Blow out the sun, turn the moon into blood!
Come back angels, bolt the door,
The time that's been will be no more!"

Go Tell It on the Mountain

THE COMPELLING LYRICS OF THIS SPIRITUAL HAVE MADE IT A POPULAR *contemporary Christmas carol. James Baldwin chose its refrain for the title of his first novel, a story based on his early experiences as a child preacher in a Pentecostal storefront church in Harlem.*

When I was a seeker,
I sought both night and day.
I asked the Lord to help me
And he showed me the way.

Go tell it on the mountain,
Over the hills and everywhere,
Go tell it on the mountain,
That Jesus Christ is Lord.

He made me a watchman,
Upon a city wall.
And if I am a Christian,
I am the least of all.

Baptizing

SLAVES HAD THEIR OWN RELIGIOUS LEADERS, CEREMONIES, AND RITUALS. *This spiritual is apparently a hymn to inaugurate and introduce a baptismal service, probably held secretly at a stream or river, away from the eyes of the slaveholders. Initiation rites and the symbolism of cleansing water were familiar institutions carried over from African culture.*

Baptizing begin,
Baptizing begin,
O! hallelujah!
Baptizing begin,
Baptizing begin.
O halle, O halle, O hallelujah!

John came down to the waterside
To examine poor sinners
And see what he'd find.

O, Jesus came down to this sinful earth,
For to save God's children
From the pains of Hell.

O, get your religion and get it now,
For the day is coming
You'll appear at the judgment bar.

I'm a Rolling

For the slaves, there was truly "an unfriendly world." Facing *a life of permanent, uncompensated toil, they kept on keeping on, kept on surviving, kept on "rolling." Theirs was a communal, not merely an individual, effort, as brothers, sisters, and preachers were urged to "help me in the service of the Lord."*

I'm a roll-ing, I'm a roll-ing, I'm a roll-ing thro' an un-

friend-ly world, I'm a roll-ing, I'm a roll-ing thro' an

un-friend-ly world.
1. O brothers, wont you help me,
2. O sis-ters, wont you help me,
3. O preachers, wont you help me,

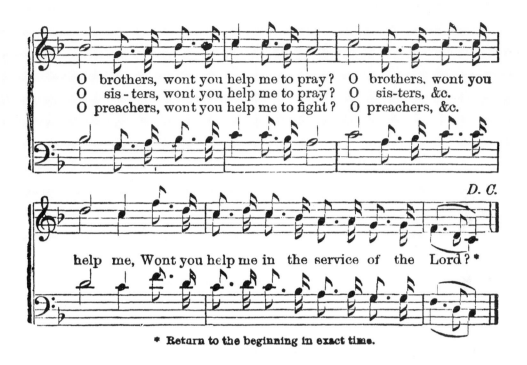

O brothers, wont you help me to pray? O brothers, wont you
O sis-ters, wont you help me to pray? O sis-ters, &c.
O preachers, wont you help me to fight? O preachers, &c.

D. C.

help me, Wont you help me in the service of the Lord?*

* Return to the beginning in exact time.

Just Above My Head

THIS CHARMING SPIRITUAL OF DIVINE AFFIRMATION SURVIVED TO BE-
come one of the inspiring songs of the modern Civil Rights movement. The reworked
lyrics proclaimed, "Just above my head / I hear freedom in the air."

Just above my head,
I hear music in the air;
Just above my head,
I hear music in the air;

Just above my head,
I hear music in the air;
There must be a God somewhere.

Do Lord, Remember Me

THE SPIRITUALS ARE COMMUNAL SONGS IN WHICH THE LEADER AND THE rest of the singers interact. *This practice comes partially from the African pattern of call-and-response antiphony and partly from the Protestant tradition of repeating the lines of hymns. We see this intimacy carry over into early jazz, where the soloist and other members of the band—almost intuitively, it seems—play with and against each other.*

Do Lord, do Lord, do remember me,
Do Lord, do Lord, do remember me,
Do Lord, do Lord, do remember me,
When I'm sick and by myself,
Do remember me;
When I'm sick and by myself,
Do remember me.
When I'm sick and by myself,
Do remember me,
Do Lord, remember me.

When I'm crossing Jordan,
Do remember me;
If I ain't got no friends at all,
Do remember me;
Paul and Silas bound in jail,
Do remember me;
One did sing while the other one prayed,
Do remember me;
When I'm bound in trouble,
Do remember me;
When I'm goin' from door to door,
Do remember me.

Don't Be Weary, Traveler

SPEAKING OF THE SPIRITUALS, THE NOVELIST AND ACTIVIST JAMES *Weldon Johnson declared, "Aframerican folk art, an art by Africans out of America, Negro creative genius, working under spur and backlash of American conditions, is unlike anything else in America or elsewhere, nor could it have been possible in any other place or in other times." This spiritual with its levels of meaning reflects that art.*

Don't be weary, traveler,
Come along home to Jesus;
Don't be weary, traveler, traveler,
Come along home to Jesus.

My head got wet with the midnight dew,
Angels bear me witness too;
Where to go I did not know

Ever since He freed my soul;
I look at the world and the world looks new,
I look at the world and the world looks new.

Don't be weary, traveler,
Come along home to Jesus;
Don't be weary, traveler, traveler,
Come along home to Jesus.

Down on Me

SLAVES LIVED LIVES OF CONSTANT WORK AND SUFFERING WITH NO *place to turn for respite or justice, since by law their masters owned their bodies as well as their labor. Survival itself was a miracle for those who lamented, "Sometimes I'm almost on the ground."*

Down on me, down on me,
Looks like everybody in the whole round
    world
Is down on me.

Talk about me as much as you please,
I'll talk about you when I get on my knees;
Sometimes I'm up, sometimes I'm down,

Sometimes I'm almost on the ground;
Heaven's so high, I am so low,
Don't know if I'll ever get to Heaven or no.

Looks like everybody in the whole round
    world
Is down on me.

Ezekiel Saw the Wheel

THE BIBLICAL SYMBOL OF EZEKIEL'S WHEEL IS ONE OF MANY IMAGES IN *the spirituals having to do with movement and transport. Chariots, trains, and shoes are some of the others. For slaves, constricted by law in their movements, to be able to travel meant being empowered to escape slavery and return home to Africa or to free themselves by running away to the North.*

Wheel, O, wheel,
Wheel in the middle of a wheel;
Wheel, O, wheel,
Wheel in the middle of a wheel.

Ezekiel saw the wheel of time,
Every spoke was humankind;
Way up on the mountaintop,
My Lord spoke and the chariot stopped.

Ezekiel saw the wheel,
Way up in the middle of the air;
Ezekiel saw the wheel,
Way up in the middle of the air.

The big wheel runs by faith,
The little wheel runs by the grace of God;
Wheel in a wheel,
Way up in the middle of the air.

Fare You Well

THIS SPIRITUAL MIGHT HAVE BEEN SUNG AT THE CONCLUSION OF A *praise service, or to say good-bye to a dying slave or perhaps to a slave about to run away. The lines "Master Jesus gave me a little broom / To sweep my heart clean" are black vernacular poetry at its very best.*

O, fare you well, my brother,
Fare you well by the grace of God,
For I'm going home;
I'm going home, my Lord,

I'm going home.
Master Jesus gave me a little broom,
To sweep my heart clean,
Sweep it clean by the grace of God,
And glory in my soul.

Fix Me, Jesus

"FIX ME, JESUS" IS A POWERFUL AFRICAN-AMERICAN IMAGE, BOTH poetically and religiously. However oppressed and cast down, the slaves sang songs of faith, confident that Jesus could "fix me so I can stand."

O, fix me, Jesus, fix me right.
Fix me right, fix me right;
O, fix me, Jesus, fix me right,
Fix me so I can stand.

O, place my feet on solid ground,
O, place my feet of solid ground;
O, when I die, you must bury me deep,
O, when I die, you must bury me deep;

O, dig my grave with a silver spade,
O, dig my grave with a silver spade;
And let me down with a golden chain,
And let me down with a golden chain.

O, fix me, Jesus, fix me right,
Fix me right, fix me right;
O, fix me, Jesus, fix me right,
Fix me so I can stand.

There's No Hiding Place Down There

THE UNKNOWN SLAVE POETS USED RICH AND VIVID IMAGERY IN THEIR lyrics. Here, when the sinner in Hell tries to find relief by running to a rock "to hide my face," the rock itself cries out, "No hiding place," and agonizes, "I'm burning, too."

There's no hiding place down there,
There's no hiding place down there.

O, I went to the rock to hide my face,
The rock cried out, "No hiding place."
There's no hiding place down there.

O, the rock cried, "I'm burning, too,"
O, the rock cried, "I'm burning, too,"
O, the rock cried, "I'm burning, too,"

I want to go to Heaven as well as you,
There's no hiding place down there.

O, the sinner man, he gambled and fell,
O, the sinner man, he gambled and fell,
O, the sinner man, he gambled and fell;
He wanted to go to Heaven,
But he had to go to Hell.
There's no hiding place down there.

He's the Lily of the Valley

THE SLAVE POET BEGINS BY REFERRING TO JESUS AS "THE LILY OF THE *valley,*" *a biblical image of beauty from Song of Solomon 2:1. But the poet goes on to describe shoes that let one "ride upon the air," symbolizing movement, travel, and escape. King Jesus, the protector of his people, is thus linked with flight from oppression.*

He's the li - ly of the val - ley, Oh! my Lord; He's the li - ly of the val - ley, Oh, my Lord;

1. King Je - sus in the cha-riot rides, Oh! my Lord; With

four white hors-es side by side, Oh! my Lord.

What kind of shoes are those you wear,
  O! my Lord;
That you can ride upon the air,
  O! my Lord.

Chorus: He's the lily of the valley . . .

These shoes I wear are gospel shoes,
  O! my Lord;
And you can wear them if you choose,
  O! my Lord.

Chorus: He's the lily of the valley . . .

Come Here, Jesus, If You Please

THE TEXT OF THE SPIRITUALS IS ORGANIC. THERE ARE NO ATTRIBUTED *authors, no fixed words, no final authoritative text. Nothing was written down. The songs were sung across the plantation South, with the same phrases turning up in different spirituals and lyrics varying from place to place. Spirituals were truly a living poetry, rooted in the experiences and sentiments of slave life. For example, there are other versions of these lyrics, which appeared in different geographic areas.*

No harm have I done you on my knees,
No harm have I done you on my knees.

O, Lord, have mercy on poor me,
O, Lord, have mercy on poor me.

When you see me on my knees,
Come here, Jesus, if you please.

I Am Not Afraid to Die

WHETHER COPING WITH THE RISKS OF LIFE AS A SLAVE OR CHANCING *the dangers of escape, slaves were constantly confronted with death. Yet the slave community never relinquished faith in the divine promise of freedom and justice, nor lost sight of the difference between Jesus and Satan, between good and evil in the slaveholding world, between the heroic milk-white horse and the Devil's iron gray.*

I am not afraid to die,
I am not afraid to die,
I am not afraid to die,
Jesus rides the milk-white horse.
I am not afraid to die.

Satan rides the iron gray,
Satan rides the iron gray,
I am not afraid to die.

I am bound for the Promised Land,
I am bound for the Promised Land,
I am not afraid to die.

I Feel Like My Time Ain't Long

THE COMPOSER VY HIGGINSEN POINTS OUT THAT ANYONE CAN SING *spirituals because these songs draw on the singers' own personal emotional experiences. This song, with its images of death, discouragement, and the fragility of life, expresses universal feelings.*

Went to the graveyard the other day,
I looked at the place where my mother lay;
Sometimes I'm up, sometimes I'm down,
And sometimes I'm almost on the ground,
Mind out, my brother, how you walk on the
    cross,
Your foot might slip and your soul get lost.

I feel like, I feel like,
I feel like my time ain't long;
I feel like, I feel like,
I feel like my time ain't long.

I Got a New Name

NEW NAMES, SYMBOLIZING THE REALITY OF NEW IDENTITIES, ARE NOT *uncommon in religious conversion. Here the singers claim the new names that will be theirs "over in Zion" (God's kingdom either on earth or in Heaven), along with the reunion of families separated by the slave system.*

I got a new name over in Zion,
I got a new name over in Zion,
I got a new name over in Zion,
Well, it's mine, mine, mine,
I declare it's mine.

I got a mother over in Zion,
I got a mother over in Zion,
I got a mother over in Zion,
Well, she's mine, mine, mine,
I declare she's mine.

I got a father over in Zion,
I got a father over in Zion,
I got a father over in Zion,
Well, he's mine, mine, mine,
I declare he's mine.

I got a new name over in Zion,
I got a new name over in Zion,
I got a new name over in Zion,
Well, it's mine, mine, mine,
I declare it's mine.

Nobody Knows the Trouble I See, Lord!

THE MUSICIAN AND CRITIC CHARLES CAMERON WHITE CLAIMS THAT *this song was written by a slave whose wife and children were sold away from him. W. E. B. Du Bois says that following the Civil War freedpeople sang it in despair over the government's refusal to provide them with land that would provide economic self-sufficiency. Whatever the song's origins, its trust in Jesus signals the triumph of faith over adversity and affirms, as Martin Luther King, Jr., has commented on this spiritual, that "no midnight long remains."*

No-bo-dy knows the trouble I see, Lord, No-bo-dy knows the

trou-ble I see, No-bo-dy knows the trouble I see, Lord,

No-bo-dy knows like Je-sus. 1. Broth-ers, will you

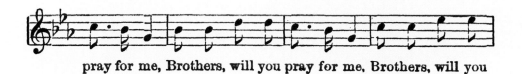

pray for me, Brothers, will you pray for me, Brothers, will you

D. C.

pray for me, And help me to drive old Sa-tan a-way.

Sisters, will you pray for me? . . .
Mothers, will you pray for me? . . .
Preachers, will you pray for me? . . .

I'm a Troubled in the Mind

AS A VERNACULAR ART FORM, SPIRITUALS HAVE THEIR OWN STORY TO *tell about life in slavery. Yet Nell Irvin Painter, the biographer of Sojourner Truth, points out that historians are not trained to understand and use musical materials, so spirituals are often not considered in the study of American or even African-American history.*

I am a-troubled in the mind,
O, I am a-troubled in the mind,

I ask my Lord what shall I do,
I am a-troubled in the mind.

I'm a-troubled in the mind,
What you doubt for?
I'm a-troubled in the mind.

I Know the Lord's Laid His Hands on Me

THIS HYMN OF FAITH AFFIRMS THE SINGER'S RELATIONSHIP TO THE
*Lord, who has blessed him with the laying on of hands. A slave's life was one
of unmitigated desperation, so faith in the Lord understandably offered hope
and help.*

O, I know the Lord, I know the Lord,
I know the Lord's laid His hands on me.

Did ever you see the like before?
Jesus preaching to the poor;
O, wasn't that a happy day?
Jesus washed my sins away;
Some seek the Lord and don't seek Him
   right,

Fool all day and pray all night;
My Lord's done just what He said,
Healed the sick and raised the dead.

O, I know the Lord, I know the Lord,
I know the Lord's laid His hands on me.

O, Sinner Man!

THOUGH MANY NINETEENTH-CENTURY CRITICS DISPARAGED THE SPIR-
*ituals as merely derivative, it is now generally conceded that they constitute the
most important and authentic American, as well as African-American, folk music.
Songs like "O, Sinner Man!" have no real parallel in European folk songs.*

O, sinner! O, sinner man!
O, sinner! O, which way are you going?

O, come back, sinner,
And don't go there,
Which way are you going?
For Hell is deep and dark despair,
O, which way are you going?

Though days be dark and nights be long,
We'll shout and sing till we get home;
'Twas just about the break of day,
My sins forgiven and soul set free.

O, sinner! O, sinner man!
O, sinner! O, which way are you going?

I Will Overcome

THIS SPIRITUAL, WHICH IS PROBABLY BASED ON THE OLD METHODIST *hymn "I'll Overcome Someday," was adapted as "We Shall Overcome" in modern times. It was first used by striking African-American members of the Food and Tobacco Workers Union in Charleston, South Carolina, in 1945. It became the signature song of the Civil Rights movement in the 1960s. Born in the hard reality of slave life and affirming the hopefulness of the oppressed, this song has spread around the world since the 1960s and has been sung by protesters from South Africa to China.*

I will overcome,
I will overcome,
I will overcome,
I will overcome,
Down in my heart,
I do believe
I will overcome someday.

Jesus take me by the hand,
Jesus take me by the hand,
Jesus take me by the hand,
Jesus take me by the hand,
Down in my heart,
I do believe
I will overcome someday.

I will be all right,
I will be all right,
I will be all right,
I will be all right,
Down in my heart,
I will overcome someday.

I will see the Lord,
I will see the Lord,
I will see the Lord,
I will see the Lord,
Down in my heart,
I do believe
I will see the Lord someday.

If You Want to See Jesus

THE AFRICAN-AMERICAN MUSICIAN QUINCY JONES WRITES, "THE TRUE *history of blacks is not in the history books but in our music." Reading between the lines of this spiritual, one sees a people captured in the wilderness of slavery but finding a way to transcend their oppression by "leaning on the Lord."*

If you want to see Jesus,
Go in the wilderness,
Go in the wilderness,
Go in the wilderness;
If you want to see Jesus,
Go in the wilderness,
Leaning on the Lord.

O, brother, how do you feel,
When you come out the wilderness?
I felt so happy,

When I come out the wilderness,
I heard the angels singing.
When I come out the wilderness,
I heard the harps a-harping.
When I come out the wilderness.

I heard the angels moaning,
When I come out the wilderness,
I gave the Devil a battle,
When I come out the wilderness,
Leaning on the Lord.

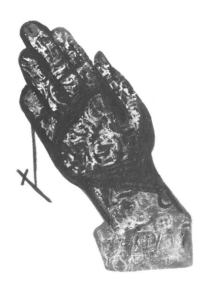

It's Me, O Lord

MANY SPIRITUALS SUGGEST THAT SLAVEHOLDERS, WITH THEIR ARRO-
*gance and cruelty, would suffer at the hands of an angry and just God. Even so, the
slaves themselves knew no spiritual pride and took full personal responsibility as
people "standing in the need of prayer."*

It's me, it's me, it's me, O Lord,
Standing in the need of prayer,
It's me, it's me, it's me, O Lord,
Standing in the need of prayer.

'Tain't my mother or my father,
But it's me, O Lord,
Standing in the need of prayer.

'Tain't my deacon or my leader,
But it's me, O Lord,
Standing in the need of prayer.

I've Been Trying to Live Humble

THOMAS WENTWORTH HIGGINSON, THE RADICAL ABOLITIONIST AND
*commander of African-American troops during the Civil War, wrote of the spiritu-
als that with slavery's end "history cannot afford to lose this portion of its record."
Spirituals like this one reveal the deeply personal quality of religion for the slaves.*

Humble, humble,
I've been trying to live humble, humble;
Ever since my soul's been converted,
I've been trying to live humble, humble.

My sister, humble up and humble down,
My brother, humble through and humble
   'round;
Humble, humble,
I've been trying to live humble, humble;
Ever since my soul's been converted,
I've been trying to live humble, humble.

Ride On, King Jesus

OF THE SEVERAL BIBLICAL IMAGES OF JESUS, THE SPIRITUALS OFTEN *chose the symbol of king, the ruler who rights what is wrong and protects his people. This image empowered the slaves, enabling them to say, "No man can a-hinder me."*

King Jesus rides on a milk-white horse,
    No man can a-hinder me;
The river of Jordan He did cross,
    No man can a-hinder me.

Chorus: Ride on . . .

If you want to find your way to God,
    No man can a-hinder me;
The gospel highway must be tred,
    No man can a-hinder me.

Chorus: Ride on . . .

Blind Man Lying at the Pool

THE AFRICAN-AMERICAN WRITER ZORA NEALE HURSTON CLAIMS THAT *no audience has ever heard real spirituals. She means that those songs formally arranged for the concert stage were merely adaptations of the authentic songs sung by and for the people themselves. For example, the phrase "O Lord save me" is a highly personal expression, one that was originally sung among a private group of worshippers, not in public performance.*

Blind man lying at the pool,
Blind man lying at the pool,
Blind man lying at the pool,
Blind man lying at the pool.

Lying there for to be healed,
Lying there for to be healed,
Lying there for to be healed,
Blind man lying at the pool.

Crying: O Lord save me,
Crying: O Lord save me,
Crying: O Lord save me,
Blind man lying at the pool.

Save my weary soul,
Save my weary soul,
Save my weary soul,
Blind man lying at the pool.

Pray remember me,
Pray remember me,
Pray remember me,
Blind man lying at the pool.

Jesus' Blood Done Make Me Whole

THE SLAVES ADAPTED THE CHARACTERISTICS OF EVANGELICAL CHRISTIANITY *to their African roots. They emphasized the transforming power of the gospel: everything changes with the experience of Jesus. It is no longer possible to "walk like I used to walk."*

Jesus' blood done make me whole,
Jesus' blood done make me whole,
Since I touched the hem of His garment,
Jesus' blood done make me whole.

I don't feel like I used to feel,
I don't feel like I used to feel,
Since I touched the hem of His garment,
I don't feel like I used to feel.

I don't mourn like I used to mourn;
I don't walk like I used to walk,
I don't talk like I used to talk,
I don't sing like I used to sing.

Jesus' blood done make me whole,
Jesus' blood done make me whole,
Since I touched the hem of His garment,
Jesus' blood done make me whole.

Listen to the Lambs

IN THE BIBLE LAMBS FREQUENTLY SYMBOLIZE THE PEOPLE OF GOD. THE *plaintive cries of young animals would be familiar to plantation workers, who also saw themselves under the protective care of the Good Shepherd.*

Listen to the lambs,
Listen to the lambs,
Listen to the lambs all a-crying,
I want to go to Heaven when I die.

Come on sister with your ups and downs,
Angels waiting for to give you a crown;
Come on sister, and don't be ashamed,

Angels waiting to write your name;
Mind out brother how you walk on the
    cross,
Foot might slip and your soul get lost.
Listen to the lambs,
Listen to the lambs,
Listen to the lambs all a-crying,
I want to go to Heaven when I die.

Let Us Break Bread Together

Originally a secret call to a clandestine religious meeting, this spiritual continues to be used as a Communion hymn in Protestant churches. Its simplicity is as direct and powerful as the elements of the Eucharist. The phrase "with my face to the rising sun" may be an Islamic retention from Africa.

Let us break bread together on our knees;
Let us break bread together on our knees;
When I fall on my knees, with my face to
  the rising sun,
O Lord, have mercy on me.

Let us drink wine together on our knees;
Let us drink wine together on our knees;
When I fall on my knees, with my face to
  the rising sun,
O Lord, have mercy on me.

Let us praise God together on our knees;
Let us praise God together on our knees;
When I fall on my knees, with my face to
  the rising sun,
O Lord, have mercy on me.

O, Mary, Don't You Weep

In this spiritual there is no need for the tears of suffering, because oppression has already been overcome. Just as the children of Israel were delivered from Pharaoh, so "one of these mornings" the slave poet is "gonna take my wings and cleave the air," escaping from bondage.

O, Mary, don't you weep, don't you moan,
O, Mary, don't you weep, don't you moan,
Pharaoh's army already got drowned,
O, Mary, don't you weep.

One of these mornings bright and fair,
Gonna take my wings and cleave the air,
Pharaoh's army already got drowned,
O, Mary don't you weep.

Lord, I Want to Be a Christian

THESE TOUCHING LYRICS TRANSCEND THE SLAVES' BITTER EXPERIENCE and speak to—and for—anyone who yearns "to be more loving" and "to be a Christian." Living amid the hypocrisy of purportedly religious slaveholders, the slaves prayed for true and honest personal faith—"in-a my heart."

Lord, I want to be a Christian,
In-a my heart, in-a my heart,
Lord, I want to be a Christian,
In-a my heart, in-a my heart.

Lord, I want to be more loving,
In-a my heart, in-a my heart;

Lord, I want to be more holy,
In-a my heart, in-a my heart;
Lord, I don't want to be like Judas,
In-a my heart, in-a my heart;
Lord, I want to be like Jesus,
In-a my heart, in-a my heart.

O, Poor Little Jesus

MANY SPIRITUALS FOCUS ON THE INFANT JESUS, THE CHILD'S INNOCENCE and vulnerability, and underline the sad fact that "this world gonna break Your heart." The destruction of childhood innocence, a state of constant vulnerability, and the heartbreaking reality of the world were all too familiar to the men and women held in slavery.

O, poor little Jesus,
O, poor little Jesus,
O, poor little Jesus,
This world gonna break Your heart,
There'll be no place to lay Your head, my
    Lord.

O, Mary she bow down and cry,
O, Mary she bow down and cry,
For there's no place to lay His head.

O, poor little Jesus,
O, poor little Jesus.

Come down all you holy angels,
Sing 'round Him with your golden harps,
For someday He will die to save this world.

O, poor little Jesus,
O, poor little Jesus.

Nobody Knows Who I Am

SLAVES WERE SUBJECTED TO PERSONAL ANONYMITY AND INVISIBILITY. *They were permitted no last names, no marriages, no recognition of parenthood. The great nineteenth-century African-American leader Frederick Douglass remarked that he never met a slave who even knew his or her own birthday. Those who poignantly sang "Nobody knows who I am" looked forward to the judgment morning, when their dehumanization would cease and they would be welcomed by name into God's kingdom.*

O, nobody knows who I am,
Who I am till the judgment morning!
Heaven bells a-ringing, the saints all
   a-singing,
Heaven bells a-ringing in my soul.

Want to go to Heaven, want to go right,
Want to go to Heaven all dressed in white;
Don't want to stumble, don't want to fall,
Want to be in Heaven when the roll is called;
If you don't believe that I've been
   redeemed,
Follow me down to Jordan's stream.

Poor Sinner, Fare You Well

THE INTERRACIAL EVANGELICAL CAMP MEETINGS OF EARLY FRONTIER *America, with their days and nights of preaching and singing, were deeply influenced from the outset by African-American participants. At the slaves' own communal worship, the praying ground was a secluded and secret spot away from the master's control, where men and women could worship in their own way.*

Big camp meeting on the praying ground,
Big camp meeting on the praying ground,
Big camp meeting on the praying ground,
Poor sinner, fare you well.

Don't you feel happy on the praying
    ground?
Don't you feel happy on the praying
    ground?
Don't you feel happy on the praying
    ground?
Poor sinner, fare you well.

I got my religion on the praying ground,
I got my religion on the praying ground,
I got my religion on the praying ground,
Poor sinner, fare you well.

I feel a little better on the praying ground,
I feel a little better on the praying ground,
I feel a little better on the praying ground,
Poor sinner, fare you well.

Is a mighty shouting on the praying ground,
Is a mighty groaning on the praying ground,
My soul got happy on the praying ground,
Poor sinner, fare you well.

Rock-a My Soul

VISITING A RELIGIOUS SERVICE FOR SLAVES IN THE 1850s, LANDSCAPE architect Frederick Law Olmsted was "surprised to find my own muscles all stretched, as if ready for a struggle—my face glowing, and my feet stamping." The presence of the spirit and the contagious enthusiasm in the church had rocked even a staid gentleman.

Rock-a my soul in the bosom of Abraham,
Rock-a my soul in the bosom of Abraham,
Rock-a my soul in the bosom of Abraham,
O, rock-a my soul.

I never shall forget the day,
When Jesus washed my sins away,
I know my God is a man of war,
He fought my battle at Hell's dark door;
If you don't believe I'm a child of God,
Follow me where the road is hard.

One day, one day I was walking nigh,
Yes, I heard a reason from on high;

I remember the day, I remember it well,
My sins were forgiven and my soul saved
    from Hell.
I went down to the valley and didn't go to
    stay,
My soul got happy and I stayed all day;
Just look up yonder what I see,
A band of angels coming after me,
If you get there before I do,
Tell my Lord I'm coming too.
When I get to Heaven and sit right down,
O, rock-a my soul,
I'll ask my Lord for my starry crown,
O, rock-a my soul.

I'm New-Born Again

THIS HYMN, WITH ITS STRIKING PHRASE "FREE GRACE AND DYING LOVE," *epitomizes the evangelical faith the slaves adapted from Protestant Christianity. The cry "I know my Lord has set me free" affirms the interior freedom of salvation, setting the deepest kind of liberty against the oppression of the slave system.*

I found free grace and dying love,
I'm new-born again,
I know my Lord has set me free,
I'm new-born again;
My Savior died for you and me,
I'm new-born again.

Been a long time talking about my trials here
  below,
Free grace, free grace, free grace.
Sinner, free grace, I been born again,
So glad! So glad! I'm new-born again,
Been a long time talking about my trials here
  below.

This Old-Time Religion

THIS POPULAR SPIRITUAL, WHICH BECAME AN EVANGELICAL GOSPEL *song, affirms the religious nature of the spirituals. As the third verse clearly states, it is "this old-time religion" that brings the enslaved out of bondage in the Jewish and Christian tradition of liberation.*

Oh! this old time re-li-gion, This old time re-li-gion, This

old time re-li-gion, It is good e-nough for me.

1. It is good for the mourner, It is good for the mourner, It is

good for the mourner, It is good e-nough for me.

It will carry you home to Heaven,
It will carry you home to Heaven,
It will carry you home to Heaven,
   It is good enough for me.

Chorus: O, this old-time religion.

It brought me out of bondage . . .

Chorus: O, this old-time religion.

It is good when you are in trouble . . .

Chorus: O, this old-time religion.

Rolling in Jesus' Arms

THE STRUCTURE OF THIS SPIRITUAL SUGGESTS THAT IT MAY HAVE BEEN *based on a hymn, but "I'm a-rolling in Jesus' arms" is a distinctive African-American phrase. It reappears later in a more secular form in a blues song—"I'm a-rolling in my sweet baby's arms."*

I'm a-rolling in Jesus' arms,
I'm a-rolling in Jesus' arms,
On the other side of Jordan,
I'm a-rolling in Jesus' arms.

One day when I was walking,
Along that lonesome road,
My Savior spoke unto me,
And filled my heart with love.

He chose me for a watchman,
To blow the trumpet of God,
To join the weary traveler
Along that heavenly road.

Why do you tarry, sinner,
Why do you wait so long?
Your Savior is a-waiting for you,
Why don't you come along?

You need not look for riches,
Nor either dress so fine,
The robe that Jesus gives you,
Outshines the glittering sun.

Somebody's Knocking at Your Door

BASED ON JESUS' WORDS IN THE NEW TESTAMENT, "BEHOLD, I STAND *at the door and knock," this spiritual calls the sinner to answer and repent. Elements of "Somebody's Knocking" were used by Antonín Dvořák in his* New World Symphony.

Somebody's knocking at your door,
Somebody's knocking at your door;
O, sinner, why don't you answer?
Somebody's knocking at your door.

Knocks like Jesus,
Knocks like Jesus;
Can't you hear Him?

Can't you hear Him?
Answer Jesus,
Answer Jesus,
Jesus calls you,
Jesus calls you;
Can't you trust Him?
Can't you trust Him?

Turn, Sinner

THE EARLIEST SPIRITUALS FOLLOWED THE AFRICAN CALL-AND-RESPONSE *model: a leader sings the first line and the rest of the group, in chorus, comes back with the second line. This model can also be found in African-American preaching. In fluid and flexible spirituals one may have any number of verses depending on the creativity of the group.*

Turn, sinner, turn,
Turn, sinner, turn,
While your Maker asks you to turn,
O, turn, sinner, turn,
May the Lord help you to turn.
O, turn, why will you die?

Pray, sinner, pray,
Pray, sinner, pray,
While your Maker asks you to pray;
Bow, sinner, bow,
Bow, sinner, bow,
While your Maker asks you to bow;
Groan, sinner, groan,
Groan, sinner, groan,
While your Maker asks you to groan.

When I'm Dead

MANY OF THE SPIRITUALS GO THROUGH A NUMBER OF VERSES LISTING *father, mother, sister, brother, deacon, and so on. The slavocracy destroyed the African family structure, separating wives and husbands, parents and children, brothers and sisters, through sales to different slaveholders. Deeply affected by these forced separations, slaves struggled to maintain family connections and memories by cataloguing family members in their songs.*

When I'm dead don't you grieve after me,
When I'm dead don't you grieve after me,
When I'm dead don't you grieve after me,
By and by don't you grieve after me.

Pale horse and rider have taken my mother
  away,
Pale horse and rider have taken my mother
  away,
Pale horse and rider have taken my mother
  away,
By and by don't you grieve after me.

Pale horse and rider stop at every door,
Pale horse and rider stop at every door,
Pale horse and rider stop at every door,
By and by don't you grieve after me.

Cold, icy hand took my father away,
Cold, icy hand took my father away,
Cold, icy hand took my father away,
By and by don't you grieve after me.

When the Train Comes Along

ALTHOUGH THIS IS OSTENSIBLY A SONG ABOUT DEATH, WE KNOW THAT *the train is a symbol of movement and therefore of escape. One might imagine Harriet Tubman, who made many dangerous trips into the South to bring out slaves through the Underground Railroad, casually singing this spiritual. Its code words "I will meet you at the station" would have communicated her presence and signaled that it was time to escape and board the "train" to freedom.*

When the train comes along,
When the train comes along,
I will meet you at the station
When the train comes along.

If my mother asks for me,
Tell her death summons me;
If my brother asks for me,
Tell him death summons me;
O, I may be blind and cannot see.

When the train comes along,
When the train comes along,
I will meet you at the station
When the train comes along.

Songs of
freedom

Go Down, Moses

"GO DOWN, MOSES" IS THE BEST KNOWN OF ALL THE SPIRITUALS AND *was the first one to be written down. African-American slaves identified themselves with Israel in bondage; they saw the master class as Pharaoh, the South as Egypt, and their own leaders, like the insurrectionist Nat Turner, as Moses. This hymn may even have been composed to honor Turner's revolt in Virginia in 1831. With the stirring words "Let my people go," this spiritual was so direct that its singing was banned on some plantations.*

1. When Is - rael was in E-gypt's land: Let my people go,

Oppress'd so hard they could not stand, Let my peo-ple go.

Go down, Mo - ses, Way down in E - gypt land,

Tell ole Pha - roh. Let my peo - ple go.

Thus saith the Lord, bold Moses said,
   Let my people go;
If not I'll smite your first-born dead,
   Let my people go.
      Go down, Moses . . .

No more shall they in bondage toil,
   Let my people go;
Let them come out with Egypt's spoil,
   Let my people go.
      Go down, Moses . . .

When Israel out of Egypt came,
   Let my people go;
And left the proud oppressive land,
   Let my people go.
      Go down, Moses . . .

O, 'twas a dark and dismal night,
   Let my people go;
When Moses led the Israelites,
   Let my people go.
      Go down, Moses . . .

'Twas good old Moses and Aaron, too,
   Let my people go;
'Twas they that led the armies through,
   Let my people go.
      Go down, Moses . . .

The Lord told Moses what to do,
   Let my people go;
To lead the children of Israel through,
   Let my people go.
      Go down, Moses . . .

O come along, Moses, you'll not get lost,
   Let my people go;
Stretch out your rod and come across,
   Let my people go.
      Go down, Moses . . .

As Israel stood by the waterside,
   Let my people go;
At the command of God it did divide,
   Let my people go.
      Go down, Moses . . .

When they had reached the other shore,
    Let my people go;
They sang a song of triumph o'er,
    Let my people go.
        Go down, Moses . . .

Pharaoh said he would go across,
    Let my people go;
But Pharaoh and his host were lost,
    Let my people go.
        Go down, Moses . . .

O, Moses, the cloud shall cleave the way,
    Let my people go;
A fire by night, a shade by day,
    Let my people go.
        Go down, Moses . . .

You'll not get lost in the wilderness,
    Let my people go;
With a lighted candle in your breast,
    Let my people go.
        Go down, Moses . . .

Jordan shall stand up, like a wall,
    Let my people go;
And the walls of Jericho shall fall,
    Let my people go.
        Go down, Moses . . .

Your foes shall not before you stand,
    Let my people go;
And you'll possess fair Canaan's land,
    Let my people go.
        Go down, Moses . . .

'Twas just about in harvest time,
    Let my people go;
When Joshua led his host divine,
    Let my people go.
        Go down, Moses . . .

O let us all from bondage flee,
    Let my people go;
And let us all in Christ be free,
    Let my people go.
        Go down, Moses . . .

We need not always weep and moan,
    Let my people go;
And wear these slavery chains forlorn,
    Let my people go.
        Go down, Moses . . .

This world's a wilderness of woe,
    Let my people go;
O, let us on to Canaan go,
    Let my people go.
        Go down, Moses . . .

What a beautiful morning that will be,
    Let my people go;
When time breaks up in eternity,
    Let my people go.
        Go down, Moses . . .

O brethren, brethren, you'd better be
        engaged,
    Let my people go;
For the Devil he's out on a big rampage,
    Let my people go.
        Go down, Moses . . .

The Devil he thought he had me fast,
    Let my people go;
But I thought I'd break his chains at last,
    Let my people go.
        Go down, Moses . . .

O take your shoes from off your feet,
    Let my people go;
And walk into the golden street,
    Let my people go.
        Go down, Moses . . .

I'll tell you what I like the best,
    Let my people go;
It is the shouting Methodist,
    Let my people go.
        Go down, Moses . . .

I do believe without a doubt,
    Let my people go;
That a Christian has the right to shout,
    Let my people go.
        Go down, Moses . . .

Come and Go with Me

WHITE PEOPLE TENDED TO INTERPRET THE SPIRITUALS AS OTHER-
*worldly because of the repeated emphasis on Heaven. As Christians, the slaves were
citizens in Heaven rather than in this world; but whatever its religious dimension,
this spiritual is a call to escape, urging others to "Come and go with me."*

This old world is not my home,
This old world is not my home,
This old world is not my home,
O, Christian, come and go with me.

Yes, I seek my home in Heaven,
Yes, I seek my home in Heaven,
O, moaner, come and go with me.

My home is in the new Jerusalem,
My home is in the new Jerusalem,
O, sinner, come and go with me.

Yes, my home is over Jordan,
Yes, my home is over Jordan,
O, sister, come and go with me.

Ain't Going to Tarry Here

THE SPIRITUALS SUBVERTED THE SOCIAL ORDER AND SERVED AS TOOLS *of resistance against oppression. "Ain't Going to Tarry Here" is a clear call to escape, speaking to both physical and spiritual liberation. The radical freedom of the Christian Good News is affirmed here in the wonderful poetic line "I sweep my house with the gospel broom."*

Sweep it clean,
Ain't going to tarry here,
Sweep it clean,
Ain't going to tarry here.

I sweep my house with the gospel broom,
Ain't going to tarry here,
I sweep my house with the gospel broom,
Ain't going to tarry here.

Sweep it clean,
Ain't going to tarry here,
Sweep it clean,
Ain't going to tarry here.

Going to open my mouth to the Lord,
Ain't going to tarry here,
Going to open my mouth to the Lord,
Ain't going to tarry here.

O-o-o Lordy,
Ain't going to tarry here,
O-o-o Lordy,
Ain't going to tarry here.

'Cause he's digging down in the grave,
Ain't going to tarry here,
'Cause he's digging down in the grave,
Ain't going to tarry here.

The big bell's tolling in Galilee,
Ain't going to tarry here,
The big bell's tolling in Galilee,
Ain't going to tarry here.

O-o-o Lordy,
Ain't going to tarry here,
O-o-o Lordy,
Ain't going to tarry here.

Bound for Canaan Land

SPEAKING OF THIS SPIRITUAL AND OF HIS LIFE AS A SLAVE, FREDERICK *Douglass wrote, "We were at times remarkably buoyant, singing hymns and making joyous exclamations about as triumphant in their tone as if we had reached a land of freedom and safety. A keen observer might have detected in our repeated singing of 'I am bound for the land of Canaan' something more than a hope of reaching heaven. We meant to reach the North, and the North was our Canaan."*

Where're you bound?
Bound for Canaan land.
Where're you bound?
Bound for Canaan land.

O, you must not lie,
You must not steal,
You must not take God's name in vain;
I'm bound for Canaan land.

Your horse is white, your garment bright,
You look like a man of war;
Raise up your head with courage bold,
For your race is almost run.

How you know?
How you know?
Jesus told me.

Although you see me going so,
I'm bound for Canaan land;
I have hard trials here below,
I'm bound for Canaan land.

Where're you bound?
Bound for Canaan land.
Where're you bound?
Bound for Canaan land.

Don't You Let Nobody Turn You Around

THE AFRICAN-AMERICAN PHILOSOPHER CORNEL WEST SPEAKS OF BLACK *music as a kind of freedom created by an unfree people, a freedom they could revel in and use to inspire the community toward other kinds of freedom. This song of encouragement proclaims that even internal religious differences do not matter next to religious integrity. It became popular during the freedom movement of the 1960s.*

Don't you let nobody turn you around,
Turn you around, turn you around,
Don't you let nobody turn you around,
Turn you around, turn you around,
Keep the straight and narrow way.

I was at the river of Jordan,
Baptism was begun,
John baptized the multitude,
But he sprinkled narry one.
The Baptists, they go by water,
The Methodists, they go by land,
But when they get to Heaven
They'll shake each other's hand.

You may be a good Baptist,
And a good Methodist as well,
But if you ain't the pure in heart
Your soul is bound for Hell.

Don't you let nobody turn you around,
Turn you around, turn you around,
Don't you let nobody turn you around,
Turn you around, turn you around.

Down by the Riverside

THIS FAMILIAR SPIRITUAL ANTICIPATES ETERNAL PEACE, AS PEOPLE LAY *down their fighting implements and vow "to study war no more." Based on Isaiah 2:4, it is often used as a pacifist theme song or as a Christian metaphor for life in the Kingdom. But for the slave, peace takes place only "down by the riverside"—across the water, in the land of freedom, whether it is the free North, the Liberia colony, the African homeland, or Heaven.*

Going to lay down my burden,
Down by the riverside,
Down by the riverside,
Down by the riverside,
Going to lay down my burden,
Down by the riverside,
I ain't going to study war no more.

I ain't going to study war no more,
I ain't going to study war no more,
I ain't going to study war no more,
I ain't going to study war no more.

Going to lay down my sword and shield,
Down by the riverside,
Down by the riverside,
Down by the riverside,
Going to lay down my sword and shield,
Down by the riverside,
Ain't going to study war no more.

I'm going to put on my long white robe,
Down by the riverside, down by the
    riverside.
I'm going to talk with the Prince of Peace,
Down by the riverside, down by the
    riverside,
Down by the riverside,
Ain't going to study war no more.

Farewell, My Brother

FREDERICK DOUGLASS'S ESCAPE FROM BONDAGE WAS INSPIRED BY SPIR-
*ituals like this one, and he became the most famous escaped slave of the nineteenth
century. He wrote in his autobiography, "I did not, when a slave, understand the
deep meaning of these rude and apparently incoherent songs. I was myself within
the circle, so that I neither saw nor heard as those without might see and hear."*

Farewell, my brother, farewell forever,
Fare you well, my brother, now,
For I am going home.
O, good-bye, good-bye,
For I am bound to leave you,
O, good-bye, good-bye,

For I am going home.
Shake hands, shake hands,
For I am bound to leave you,
O, shake hands, shake hands,
For I am going home.

Fighting On

TO SURVIVE, THE SLAVES HAD TO MAINTAIN THEIR COURAGE, TO BELIEVE
*that the battle would continue as long as even one person was in bondage, and—in
the graphic words of this spiritual—to keep fighting on. The goal of the struggle
was an egalitarianism symbolized here in Jesus' death for "every man," and to "set
the whole world free."*

Fighting on, hallelujah,
We're almost down to the shore.
Fighting on, fighting on, hallelujah,
We're almost down to the shore.

Hallelujah to the Lamb;
Jesus died for every man.
He died for you, He died for me;
He died to set the whole world free.

In my room by my bed,
Jesus take me when I'm dead;
When I get on that other shore,
I'll bless my Lord forever more.

Fighting on, hallelujah,
We're almost down to the shore.
Fighting on, fighting on, hallalujah,
We're almost down to the shore.

Free at Last

FREEDOM IS CLEARLY THE THREAD THAT RUNS THROUGH ALL OF *African-American history. In this spiritual, as in many others, the word* freedom *refers both to salvation from sin and to liberation from the oppressive chains of American slavery. Martin Luther King, Jr., made this chorus famous when he used it at the end of his "I Have a Dream" speech at the March on Washington in 1963.*

I know my Lord is a man of war;
He fought my battle at Hell's dark door.
Satan thought he had me fast;
I broke his chain and got free at last.

Free at last, free at last,
Thank God almighty, I'm free at last.
Free at last, free at last,
Thank God almighty, I'm free at last.

You can hinder me here, but you can't
   hinder me there;
The Lord in Heaven's going to answer my
   prayer.
I went in the valley, but I didn't go to stay;
My soul got happy and I stayed all day.

God's Gonna Set This World on Fire

AFTER THE FLOOD OF NOAH'S TIME, AS RECORDED IN THE HEBREW *Bible, God threatened a sinful and unjust world with "the fire next time." This spiritual envisions a divine intervention that would destroy the world of slavery by fire. Yet the slaves themselves would be saved because God would offer them "the healing cup."*

God's gonna set this world on fire,
One of these days;
God's gonna set this world on fire,
One of these days,
O, God's gonna set this world on fire,
One of these days.

I'm gonna drink from the healing cup,
One of these days;
I'm gonna drink from the healing cup,
I'm gonna drink from the healing cup,
I'm gonna drink from the healing cup,
One of these days.

Didn't My Lord Deliver Daniel

In their oppression slaves related to those biblical figures who were saved from danger and adversity by a powerful and protective God. "Didn't My Lord Deliver Daniel" is perhaps the most politically radical of all the spirituals. It expands the idea of deliverance to encompass all the downtrodden by raising the striking, even revolutionary, question "And why not every man?"

Sung in Unison.

Did-n't my Lord de-liv-er Dan-iel, D'liver Dan-iel, d'liver Dan-iel, Did-n't my Lord de-liv-er Dan-iel, And why not a ev-e-ry man? He de-liv-er'd Dan-iel from the li-on's den, Jo-nah from the bel-ly of the whale, And the He-brew children from the

fie - ry fur-nace, And why not ev - e - ry man?

Did - n't my Lord de - liv - er Dan - iel. D'liver

Dan - iel, d'liver Dan-iel, Did - n't my Lord de - liv - er

Dan - iel, And why not a ev - e - ry man?

2D VERSE.

The moon run down in a purple-stream, The sun for - bear to

D. C. "Didn't my Lord."

shine, And ev - e - ry star dis-ap-pear, King Jesus shall be mine.

3D VERSE.

The wind blows East, and the wind blows West, It

* Go on without pause, leaving out two beats of the measure.

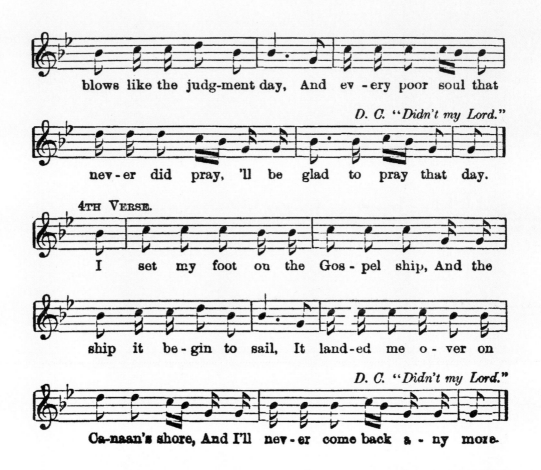

blows like the judg-ment day, And ev-ery poor soul that

D. C. "Didn't my Lord."

nev-er did pray, 'll be glad to pray that day.

4TH VERSE.

I set my foot on the Gos-pel ship, And the

ship it be-gin to sail, It land-ed me o-ver on

D. C. "Didn't my Lord."

Ca-naan's shore, And I'll nev-er come back a-ny more.

Come By Here, My Lord

As "Kuumbya," this spiritual has become a popular campfire song. For the slaves, it was a call to God to help those who needed him in the here-and-now. It is a moving and eloquent testimony to the this-worldliness of the spirituals.

Come by here, my Lord,
Come by here,
Come by here, my Lord,
Come by here,
Come by here, my Lord,
Come by here,
O, Lord,
Come by here.

Somebody's dying, Lord,
Come by here,
Somebody's dying, Lord,
Come by here,
Somebody's dying, Lord,
Come by here,
O, Lord,
Come by here.

Somebody's praying, Lord,
Come by here,
Somebody's praying, Lord,
Come by here,
Somebody's praying, Lord,
Come by here,
O, Lord,
Come by here.

Somebody needs you, Lord,
Come by here,
Somebody needs you, Lord,
Come by here,
Somebody needs you, Lord,
Come by here,
O, Lord,
Come by here.

God's Going to Trouble the Water

THE THEME OF THIS SPIRITUAL REFERS TO THE STORY IN THE FIFTH *chapter of John's gospel about the man who desires healing from the pool at Bethesda where God "troubles" the water, stirring it up by his divine presence. The message is that it is safe, even necessary, to step out into a "troubled" situation, even the Red Sea, because God's action in agitating events may be disruptive, but it is ultimately healing and redemptive. "Do not shrink from moving confidently out into choppy seas," the theologian Howard Thurman writes of these lyrics. It has also been suggested that this song was used by Harriet Tubman on the Underground Railroad, instructing runaways to travel by water in order to throw off pursuing bloodhounds.*

Wade in the water, children,
Wade in the water, children,
Wade in the water, children,
God's going to trouble the water.

See that host all dressed in white,
The leader looks like the Israelite;

See that band all dressed in red,
Looks like the band that Moses led.

Wade in the water, children,
Wade in the water, children,
Wade in the water, children,
God's going to trouble the water.

Going to Set Down and Rest Awhile

SLAVES HAD TO WORK FROM DAWN TO DARK, "FROM CAN SEE TO CAN'T *see," or "from daylight till unconscious," as the slaves said. It is little wonder that one reward of Heaven or of escape was "to set down and rest awhile." These lyrics also contain coded double-meanings about death and running away: those who escaped "didn't go to come back no more."*

Going to set down and rest awhile,
Going to set down and rest awhile,
Going to set down and rest awhile,
When my good Lord calls me.

Sister Mary went to Heaven,
And she went there to stay,
And she didn't go to come back no more;
She sang a song that the angels couldn't
  sing:
"Hosanna, carry on."

Little children, don't you moan,
Little children, don't you moan,
Little children, don't you moan,
When my good Lord calls me.
O, Zion!
O, Zion!
O, Zion!
When my good Lord calls me.

Great Day

THE IMAGE HERE IS OF SLAVES AS GOD'S RIGHTEOUS ARMY, AN IMAGE *that reappears in many spirituals. The battle for liberation has been won: "The Lord has set His people free." It is a "great day" for justice, and the future promises the building up of Zion, the community of God's people.*

Great day, the righteous are marching,
Great day!
God's going to build up Zion's walls.

The chariot rode on the mountaintop,
My God He spoke and the chariot stopped;
This is the day of jubilee,
The Lord has set His people free.

Going to take my breastplate, sword in
    hand,
And march out boldly in the field;
We want no cowards in our band,
We call for valiant-hearted men.

Great day, the righteous are marching,
Great day!
God's going to build up Zion's walls.

Holy, Holy, You Promised to Answer Prayer

THE SPIRITUALS ARE THE PRAYERS OF A PEOPLE IN BONDAGE, YEARNING *for freedom. They have faith in their eventual deliverance from oppression. They trust that God will answer their petitions, rescue them from the "barren land" of bondage. Just as God locked the lion's jaw when Daniel was thrown into the beast's den, God will deliver the slaves from their masters.*

Holy, holy, You promised to answer prayer,
Holy, holy, You promised to answer prayer,
In that morning when the Lord said holy.

John! John! This is a barren land,
John! John! This is a barren land;
Who locked, who locked,

Who locked the lion's jaw?
Lord, Lord, this is a needed time.

Holy, holy, You promised to answer prayer,
Holy, holy, You promised to answer prayer,
In that morning when the Lord said holy.

I Am Bound for the Promised Land

THE SPIRITUALS ARE OBSESSED WITH FREEDOM, EXPRESSING THE HOPE *for salvation both on earth and in Heaven, in this life and the next. It is important to remember that psychological or mental freedom was as important to those in bondage as physical freedom. By trying to teach the slaves they were inferior, the slaveholders sought to build a mental prison as well as a physical one. This spiritual reflects the slaves' deep defiance against mental servitude, and their own positive self-affirmation.*

I am bound for the Promised Land,
I am bound for the Promised Land,
O, won't you rise and go with me,
I am bound for the Promised Land.

When I get to Heaven I'll set and tell,
I am bound for the Promised Land,
Just how I shun the gates of Hell,
I am bound for the Promised Land.
O, Christians, Christians be enraged,
I am bound for the Promised Land,
Old Satan in an awful rage,
I am bound for the Promised Land.

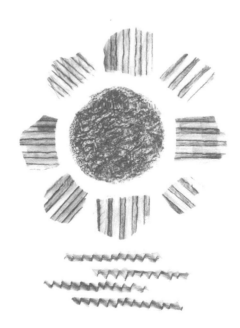

I Am Free

DESCRIBING THE SINGING OF SPIRITUALS BEFORE THE EMANCIPATION *Proclamation of 1863, Booker T. Washington wrote, "They had sung these same verses before, but they had been careful to explain that the 'freedom' in these songs referred to the next world. . . . Now they gradually threw off the mask; and were not afraid to let it be known that the 'freedom' in these songs meant freedom of the body in this world." "I Am Free" is one of those spirituals.*

I am free,
I am free, my Lord,
I am free,
I'm washed by the blood of the Lamb.

You may knock me down,
I'll rise again,
I'm washed by the blood of the Lamb;
I fight you with my sword and shield,
I'm washed by the blood of the Lamb.

Remember the day, I remember it well,
My dungeon shook and my chain fell off;
Jesus cleaned and made me white,
Said go in peace and sin no more;
Glory to God, let your faith be strong,
Lord, it won't be long before I'll be gone.

John Brown's Body

"JOHN BROWN'S BODY" MAY SEEM AN UNLIKELY SPIRITUAL, BUT BROWN *was a hero to African Americans because of his heroic attempt to incite a slave uprising at Harpers Ferry, Virginia, and his realization, eloquently expressed at his trial in 1859, that only the shedding of blood would end slavery in America. This spiritual became a popular marching song for Union troops during the Civil War. Following the Civil War, the Fisk Jubilee Singers sang it in London for the Grand Duchess Maria Fyodorovna, whose father-in-law, Czar Alexander II, had just liberated the Russian serfs.*

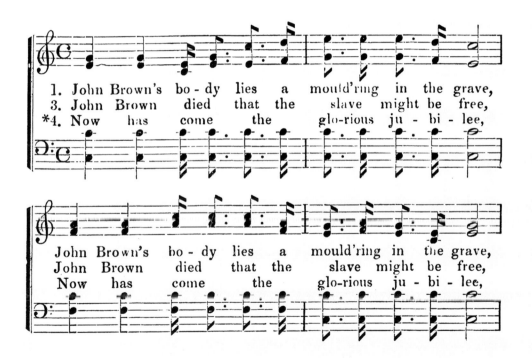

1. John Brown's bo - dy lies a mould'ring in the grave,
3. John Brown died that the slave might be free,
*4. Now has come the glo-rious ju - bi - lee,

John Brown's bo - dy lies a mould'ring in the grave,
John Brown died that the slave might be free,
Now has come the glo-rious ju - bi - lee,

John Brown's bo-dy lies a mould'ring in the grave, But his
John Brown died that the slave might be free, But his
Now has come the glo-rious ju - bi - lee, When all

soul's marching on.
soul's marching on.
man - kind are free.
Glo - ry, glo - ry Hal - le-

lu-jah, Glo-ry, glo-ry Hal-le - lu-jah, Glo - ry, glo-ry Hal-le-

lujah, His soul's marching on. 2. He captured Harper's Ferry with his

* The words of the fourth verse do not correspond fully to the notes, but the adaptation can be easily made by the singer.

nineteen men so true, And he frightened old Vir-gi-nia till she trembled through and through. They hung him for a traitor, them-selves the traitor crew, But his soul's marching on.

I Know I Would Like to Read

ILLITERACY WAS ANOTHER WAY TO KEEP MEN AND WOMEN IN BONDAGE. *Although teaching slaves to read was forbidden in the Southern states, some slaves did learn to read. They might be taught secretly by another slave, by a white child or an indulgent mistress, or they might painfully work out letters and words without instruction. Every slave could agree with this spiritual: "I know I would like to read." Following the Civil War, thousands crammed makeshift schools to acquire the literacy that had been denied them.*

I know I would like to read, like to read,
Like to read a sweet story of old,
I would like to read, like to read,
I would like to read a sweet story of old.

Come on, brother, and help me sing,
The story of King Emmanuel;
If ever I get up on the other shore,

By the grace of God I'll come here no more;
I just want to get up on the mountaintop,
I'll praise my God and never stop.

I know I would like to read, like to read,
Like to read a sweet story of old,
I would like to read, like to read,
I would like to read a sweet story of old.

I Want to Go Home

UNLIKE MOST OTHER SPIRITUALS, THIS SONG SPEAKS DIRECTLY OF THE *slave experience: the rain and hot sun of the endless days in the fields, the "hard trials," the cracking whips. It even uses the word* slavery, *asserting that it does not exist in God's kingdom. "Home" is Heaven, the free North, Africa, Canada, or the colony for manumitted slaves in Liberia.*

There's no rain to wet you,
O, yes, I want to go home,
Want to go home.

There's no sun to burn you,
O, yes, I want to go home;
There're no hard trials,
O, yes, I want to go home;
There're no whips a-cracking,

O, yes, I want to go home;
There's no tribulation,
O, yes, I want to go home;
There's no more slavery in the Kingdom,
O, yes, I want to go home;
There're no evil-doers in the Kingdom,
O, yes, I want to go home;
All is gladness in the Kingdom,
O, yes, I want to go home.

I'm Going to Tell God All My Troubles

THE AFRICAN-AMERICAN PHILOSOPHER CORNEL WEST POINTS OUT *that the spirituals, like the blues, portray a people wrestling with suffering, with the very existence of evil—wrestling in order to keep from snapping and breaking. It was a relief for the slaves to believe that God cared how his people were treated, that he would listen to "all my troubles."*

I'm going to tell God all my troubles,
I'm going to tell God all my troubles,
I'm going to tell God all my troubles,
When I get home.

I'm going to tell God how you treat me,
I'm going to tell God how you treat me,
I'm going to tell God how you treat me,
When I get home.

I'm Running for My Life

THE GRAPHIC PHRASE "I'M RUNNING FOR MY LIFE" BRINGS TO MIND THE *autobiographical narrative of Ellen and William Craft. Wearing disguises, they escaped from slavery in the Deep South in 1848 and made their dangerous way to the free North. They then sailed for England. They wrote their story in a book entitled* Running a Thousand Miles for Freedom.

I'm running for my life,
I'm running for my life,
I'm running for my life,
I'm running for my life,
I'm running for my life.

If anybody asks you what's the matter with
    me,
Just tell him I say
I'm running for my life.

I'm moaning for my life,
If anybody asks you what's the matter with
    me,
Just tell him I say
I'm moaning for my life.

I'm praying for my life.
If anybody asks you what's the matter with
    me,
Just tell him I say
I'm praying for my life.

In This Land

THE SLAVES' PROFOUND SENSE OF COMMUNITY AND THEIR BELIEF IN *God's graciousness led them to pray for all those in need "in this land." They even included liars and hypocrites in their prayers. After all, God and his universe are fundamentally just, and at the resurrection morning "we shall face another sun."*

Lord, help the poor and needy,
In this land, in this land,
Lord, help the poor and needy,
In this land, in this land.

In that great getting-up morning,
We shall face another sun.

Lord, help the widows and the orphans,
Lord, help the motherless children,
Lord, help the hypocrite members,
Lord, help the long tongue liars.

In that great getting-up morning,
We shall face another sun.

I've Been in the Storm So Long

FREDERICK DOUGLASS WROTE, "I HAVE SOMETIMES THOUGHT THAT THE *mere hearing of these songs would do more to impress some minds with the horrible character of slavery than the reading of whole volumes of philosophy on the subject could do." Listening to the personal testimony of those who have "been in the storm so long" communicates far more than any theoretical thesis on the oppression of the slave system.*

I've been in the storm so long,
I've been in the storm so long, children,
I've been in the storm so long,
O, give me little time to pray.

O, let me tell my mother
How I come along,
O, give me little time to pray,
With a hung-down head and a aching
    heart,
O, give me little time to pray.

O, when I get to Heaven,
I'll walk all about,
O, give me little time to pray.
There'll be nobody there to turn me out,
O, give me little time to pray.

I've been in the storm so long,
I've been in the storm so long, children,
I've been in the storm so long,
O, give me little time to pray.

Joshua Fit the Battle of Jericho

ONE OF THE MOST POPULAR SPIRITUALS, "JOSHUA FIT THE BATTLE OF *Jericho," shows the slaves' creative adaptation of the biblical story. The appeal lay in the image of the power of God's people, whose righteous shout brought down the walls of the city, effecting change. Mary White Ovington, one of the white founders of the National Association for the Advancement of Colored People (NAACP), chose* The Walls Came Tumbling Down *as the title of her autobiography—to herald, she hoped, the end of separation between the races.*

Joshua fit the battle of Jericho, Jericho,
   Jericho;
Joshua fit the battle of Jericho,
And the walls came tumbling down.

You may talk about your king of Gideon,
You may talk about your man of Saul;
There's none like good old Joshua
At the battle of Jericho.

Up to the walls of Jericho
He marched with spear in hand;
"Go blow the ram horns," Joshua said,
"'Cause the battle is in my hands."

Then the lamb, ram, sheep horns began to
   blow;
Trumpets began to sound;
Joshua commanded the children to shout,
And the walls came tumbling down

That morning Joshua fit the battle of
   Jericho, Jericho, Jericho;
Joshua fit the battle of Jericho,
And the walls came tumbling down.

Little David Play on Your Harp

DAVID WAS NOT ONLY A SHEPHERD, KING, MUSICIAN, AND CREATOR OF *psalms, he was also the boy who slew the giant Goliath. African-American folk songs and stories abound with accounts of the weak triumphing over the strong, giving hope to a subject people. The African-American composer William Grant Still learned this spiritual from his illiterate grandmother and incorporated it into his work.*

Little David, play on your harp,
Hallelu, Hallelujah,
Little David, play on your harp,
Hallelu.
David had a harp,
Had ten strings,
Touch one string,
And the whole Heaven ring.

David, play on your harp,
Hallelu, Hallelujah,
Little David, play on your harp,
Hallelu.

I say to David,
"Come play me a piece."
David said to me,
"How can I play, when I'm in a strange
   land?"

David, play on your harp,
Hallelu, Hallelujah,
Little David, play on your harp,
Hallelu.
David, play on your harp,
Hallelu, Hallelujah,
Little David, play on your harp,
Hallelu!

Look What a Wonder Jesus Done

MANY OF THE SPIRITUALS EMPHASIZE THE KINGSHIP OF JESUS, THE POWER *of his miracles, and the Christian faith that Christ died to redeem each sinner. Here the slave poet's direct and dramatic declaration reflects awe at the Lord's power and might. To the slaves, salvation and freedom are really the same.*

Look what a wonder Jesus done,
Sinner believe—
Look what a wonder Jesus done,
Sinner believe—
Look what a wonder Jesus done,
Sinner believe—
King Jesus had died for me.

King Jesus make the cripple walk,
Sinner believe—
King Jesus had died for me.

King Jesus gave the blind the sight,
Sinner believe—
King Jesus had died for me.

King Jesus make the dumb man speak,
Sinner believe—
King Jesus had died for me.

Look what a wonder Jesus done,
Sinner believe—
Look what a wonder Jesus done,
Sinner believe—
King Jesus had died for me.

Lord, I Cannot Stay Here by Myself

AFRICANS HAD STRONG FAMILY TIES, BUT THESE WERE DESTROYED BY *the slave system. Husbands and wives, parents and children, brothers and sisters could be separated from each other forever at any time at their master's whim. Many were left "in this world alone." This spiritual may be about death by suicide, or it may be about running away, with "the low depot" referring to a station on the Underground Railroad.*

Lord, I cannot stay here by myself, by
   myself,
Lord, I cannot stay here by myself, by
   myself.

My mother has gone and left me here,
My father has gone and left me here,
I'm going to weep like a willow
And mourn like a dove,
O Lord, I cannot stay here by myself.

Yes, I am a poor little motherless child,
Yes, I am a poor little child of God
In this world alone,
O Lord, I cannot stay here by myself.

I got my ticket at the low depot,
Low depot,
Yes, I got my ticket at the low depot,
Low depot.
Yes, I got my ticket at the low depot,
O Lord, I cannot stay here by myself.

Run to Jesus

FREDERICK DOUGLASS, THE GREAT AFRICAN-AMERICAN ABOLITIONIST *and civil rights advocate of the nineteenth century, wrote that hearing this song when he was a young slave first gave him his idea of escape, of a clandestine flight to a free state and self-emancipation out of bondage. Runaways indeed had to "shun the danger" because there were truly "lions in the way," including professional slave catchers. But they counted on Jesus, the symbol of salvation and deliverance, to be their companion along the dangerous way.*

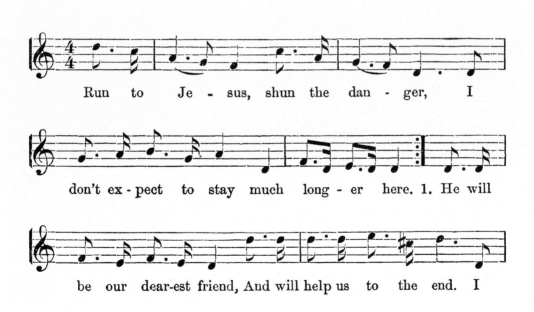

Run to Je - sus, shun the dan - ger, I
don't ex - pect to stay much long - er here. 1. He will
be our dear-est friend, And will help us to the end. I

don't ex-pect to stay much long - er here.   Run to   Je - sus,

shun the   dan - ger, I don't ex-pect to stay much long-er here.

O, I thought I heard them say,
There were lions in the way.
I don't expect . . .

Many mansions there will be,
One for you and one for me.
I don't expect . . .

No Man Can Hinder Me

THIS SPIRITUAL BEGINS WITH AN APPARENT PARADOX: JESUS IS SWEET *and kind, but he has such power that no one can thwart him. King Jesus of the milk-white horse—protective of his subjects—is so strong even the powerful, satanic slaveholders cannot defeat his will.*

Walk in, kind Savior,
No man can hinder me!
Walk in, sweet Jesus,
No man can hinder me!

See what wonder Jesus done,
Jesus make the dumb to speak,
Jesus make the cripple walk,
Jesus give the blind His sight,

Jesus do most anything.
Rise, poor Lazarus, from the tomb,
Satan ride an iron-gray horse,
King Jesus ride a milk-white horse.

Walk in, kind Savior,
No man can hinder me!
Walk in, sweet Jesus,
No man can hinder me!

My Mind Stayed on Freedom

DESPITE CONSTANT BRUTALITY, HUMILIATION, AND DEPERSONALIZATION, *somehow the slave community never lost sight of the light of freedom. After 250 years of bondage, men and women could still sing, "I woke up this morning with my mind stayed on freedom." This song came back to life in the Civil Rights movement of the 1960s.*

I woke up this morning with my mind
Stayed on freedom,
I woke up this morning with my mind
Stayed on freedom,
I woke up this morning with my mind
Stayed on freedom,
Hallelu! Hallelu! Hallelu!

My mother got her mind
Stayed on freedom,
My father got his mind
Stayed on freedom,
My brother got his mind
Stayed on freedom,
My sister got her mind
Stayed on freedom,
Hallelu! Hallelu! Hallelu!

Master Going to Sell Us Tomorrow

This spiritual speaks directly to the separation by sale of a *mother and child in a slave family. The reference to Georgia conjures up the dreaded large plantations of the Deep South, where men, women, and children were literally worked to death. Indeed, as the soil gave out in Virginia, some owners bred slave children for the market just as they did animals. When emancipation came with the Civil War, the roads were crowded with thousands of people seeking separated husbands, wives, children, brothers, sisters, and parents.*

Mother, is master going to sell us tomorrow?
Yes, yes, yes!
Mother, is master going to sell us tomorrow?
Yes, yes, yes!
Mother, is master going to sell us tomorrow?
Yes, yes, yes!
O, watch and pray!

Going to sell us down in Georgia?
Yes, yes, yes!
Going to sell us down in Georgia?
Yes, yes, yes!
O, watch and pray!

Farewell, Mother, I must leave you.
Yes, yes, yes!
Farewell, Mother, I must leave you.
Yсз, yсз, yсз!
O, watch and pray!

Mother, don't grieve after me.
No, no, no!
Mother, don't grieve after me.
No, no, no!
O, watch and pray!

Mother, I'll meet you in Heaven.
Yes, my child!
Mother, I'll meet you in Heaven.
Yes, my child!
O, watch and pray!

O, Lord, I'm Hungry

RELIGION IS RESISTANCE, AS THE AFRICAN-AMERICAN PHILOSOPHER *Alisa Bierria has pointed out, particularly when it subverts the state from below by putting God above secular power. This spiritual repeats Jesus' command to feed the hungry and clothe the naked, to care for the victims of injustice and suffering. Interestingly, the song does not include Jesus' parallel command to visit the imprisoned, perhaps because slavery had turned the whole country into a prison house.*

O, Lord, I'm hungry,
I want to be fed,
O, Lord, I'm hungry,
I want to be fed,
O, feed me, Jesus, feed me,
Feed me all my days,
O, feed me all the days of my life,
O, feed me, Jesus, feed me,
Feed me all my days,
O, feed me all the days of my life.

O, Lord, I'm naked,
I want to be clothed,
O, Lord, I'm naked,
I want to be clothed,
O, clothe me, Jesus, clothe me,

Clothe me all my days,
O, clothe me all the days of my life,
O, clothe me, Jesus, clothe me,
Clothe me all my days,
O, clothe me all the days of my life.

O, Lord, I'm sinful,
I want to be saved,
O, Lord, I'm sinful,
I want to be saved,
O, save me, Jesus, save me,
Save me all my days,
O, save me all the days of my life,
O, save me, Jesus, save me,
Save me all my days,
O, save me all the days of my life.

O, Freedom

The African-American theologian James Cone writes, "Freedom for black slaves was not a theological idea about being delivered from the oppression of sin. It was a historical reality." This classic spiritual survived to become a major song of the Civil Rights movement.

O, freedom, O, freedom,
O, freedom over me!
And before I'd be a slave,
I'll be buried in my grave,
And go home to my Lord and be free.

No more moaning, no more moaning,
No more moaning over me.
No more weeping, no more weeping,
No more weeping over me!

There'll be singing over me!
There'll be shouting, there'll be shouting,
There'll be shouting over me!
There'll be praying, there'll be praying,
There'll be praying over me.

O, freedom, O, freedom,
O, freedom over me!
And before I'd be a slave,
I'll be buried in my grave,
And go home to my Lord and be free.

You Shall Reap

The phrase "You shall reap just what you sow" reappears frequently in the lyrics of blues songs. It reflects African Americans' faith that the universe is ultimately governed by fairness and that people are responsible for their actions. Despite their undeserved pain and suffering, many slaves held on to the belief that whatever the wrongs of the present, in the end the scales of justice would be balanced.

You shall reap just what you sow,
You shall reap just what you sow,
On the mountain, in the valley,
You shall reap just what you sow.

Brother, sister, sinner,
You shall reap just what you sow,
On the mountain, in the valley,
You shall reap just what you sow.

Rise and Shine

In Marc Connelly's 1930 Pulitzer Prize—winning Broadway show, *The Green Pastures, the Hal Johnson Choir sang authentic African-American songs with dignity and beauty. Their performance saved an otherwise naive and condescending caricature of black life. This spiritual was the first number in the show. The "year of jubilee" refers to the Hebrews' practice, recorded in Leviticus 25, of freeing their slaves once every fifty years.*

O, brethren, rise and shine,
And give God the glory, glory.
Rise and shine,
And give God the glory, glory,
Rise and shine,
And give God the glory,
For the year of jubilee.

Don't you want to be a soldier, soldier,
    soldier?
Don't you want to be a soldier, soldier,
    soldier?

Do you think I will make a soldier?
Yes, I think you will make a soldier,
For the year of jubilee!

O, brethren, rise and shine,
And give God the glory, glory.
Rise and shine,
And give God the glory, glory,
Rise and shine,
And give God the glory,
For the year of jubilee.

Run, Mary, Run

JOHN LOVELL, JR., A LEADING SCHOLAR OF AFRICAN-AMERICAN SPIR-
*ituals, finds these particular lyrics revolutionary, with the references to fire and the
declaration "I know the other world is not like this." Lovell writes, "The slave just
saw too many things wrong with the existing order to hope that a few alterations
here and there would satisfy. . . . Directly or indirectly, therefore, there had to be
revolution."*

Run, Mary, run; run, Mary, run,
O, run, Mary, run.
I know the other world is not like this;
Fire in the east, and fire in the west,
I know the other world is not like this,
Bound to burn the wilderness,
I know the other world is not like this.

Jordan river is a river to cross,
I know the other world is not like this;
Stretch your rod and come across,
I know the other world is not like this.

Swing low, chariot, into the east,
Let God's children have some peace;
Swing low, chariot, into the west,
Let God's children have some rest.

Swing low, chariot, into the north,
Give me the gold without the dross;
Swing low, chariot, into the south,
Let God's children sing and shout.

If this day was judgment day,
Every sinner would want to pray;
That trouble it comes like a gloomy cloud,
Gathers thick, and thunders loud.
Run, Mary, run; run, Mary, run,
O, run, Mary, run.
I know the other world is not like this.

Steal Away

"STEAL AWAY" IS ONE OF THE MOST BEAUTIFUL SPIRITUALS, AND ITS
*lyrics can stand alone as a poem. One of the many signal songs for runaway slaves,
it used Jesus' name in a metaphor as an open invitation to escape from bondage.*

Steal a-way, steal a-way, steal a-way to Je-sus!

Steal a-way, steal a-way home, I hain't got long to stay here.

1. My Lord   calls me, He calls me by the thunder ; The
2. Green trees are bending, Poor sin-ners stand trembling ; The,&c

trumpet sounds it in my soul: I hain't got long to stay here.

My Lord calls me,
   He calls me by the lightning;
The trumpet sounds it in my soul:
   I hain't got long to stay here.

Chorus: Steal away . . .

Tombstones are bursting,
   Poor sinners are trembling;
The trumpet sounds it in my soul:
   I hain't got long to stay here.

Chorus: Steal away . . .

Sit Down

THE AFRICAN-AMERICAN THEOLOGIAN JAMES CONE WRITES, "THE *meaning of the song is not contained in the bare words but in the black history that creates it." This spiritual reflects the slaves' daily lives—their backbreaking work, their sorrow, their pain. It promises that at the end of the long journey through slavery and life, all the servants will be invited to sit down and rest at last.*

Sit down, servant; sit down, servant;
Sit down and rest a little while.
Sit down, servant; sit down, servant;
Sit down and rest a little while.

I know you are tired; sit down, servant;
You come over mountain; sit down, servant;
I know you had trouble; sit down, servant;
I know you been crying; sit down, servant.

I know you been praying; sit down, servant;
I know you been afflicted; sit down, servant;
It a tiresome journey; sit down, servant;
It a long journey; sit down, servant.

Tell All the World, John

DENA J. EPSTEIN, A MAJOR HISTORIAN OF AFRICAN-AMERICAN MUSIC, *writes that white missionaries to the slaves tried to stamp out "pagan" African music and substitute evangelical hymns, but the slaves transformed these hymns and created something new out of them. These songs criticized the slave world—"I know the other world's not like this"—and encouraged escape—"What kind of shoes are those you wear / That you can walk up in the air?"*

Tell all the world, John,
Tell all the world, John,
I know the other world's not like this.

What kind of shoes are those you wear,
That you can walk up in the air?
When Jesus shook the manna tree,
He shook it for you and He shook it for me.
Going to talk to the Father, talk to the Son,
Going to talk about the work that I left
    undone.

Slavery's Chain

ONE OF THE MOST DRAMATIC MOMENTS OF THE CIVIL WAR TOOK PLACE *at the surrender of the Confederate capital, Richmond, Virginia, in 1865. African-American federal troops marched smartly into the burning city to be met by the slave community gathered at Richmond's slave pens. Set free by black soldiers in blue uniforms on that fearful and hated spot at that very moment, the liberated men and women broke into song—and were joined by the Union troops. This is the spiritual they sang together.*

Slavery's chain done broke at last, broke at
   last, broke at last,
Slavery's chain done broke at last,
Going to praise God till I die.

Slavery's chain done broke at last, broke at
   last, broke at last,
Slavery's chain done broke at last,
Going to praise God till I die.

Slavery's chain done broke at last, broke at
   last, broke at last,
Slavery's chain done broke at last,
Going to praise God till I die.

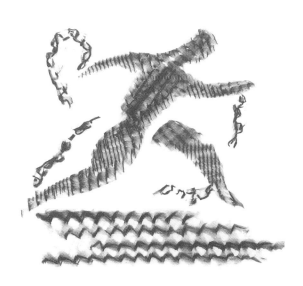

Some of These Days

FROM ITS OPENING LINE—"I'M GONNA TELL GOD HOW YOU TREAT *me*"—*this spiritual gives the lie to the white-created image of the contented slave so prevalent in nineteenth-century minstrel shows. These shows—popular among white audiences—involved performances by whites in blackface who supposedly imitated African-American singing, dancing, and humor. Minstrelsy, however, was a vicious and demeaning caricature, which helped institutionalize negative stereotypes of black people. After the Civil War, performances of spirituals like this helped to reclaim authentic African-American culture from vulgar prejudice.*

I'm gonna tell God how you treat me,
I'm gonna tell God how you treat me,
Some of these days. Hallelujah!
I'm gonna tell God how you treat me,
I'm gonna tell God how you treat me,
Some of these days.

I'm gonna cross the river of Jordan;
I'm gonna drink of the healin' waters;
I'm gonna drink and never get thirsty;
I'm gonna eat off the welcome table;
I'm gonna walk and talk with Jesus;
I'm gonna ride in the chariot with Jesus;
I'm gonna shout and not be weary;
You're gonna wish that you'd-a been ready;
God's gonna set your sins before you;
God's gonna bring this world to judgment;
Some of these days. Hallelujah!
Some of these days.

That Lonesome Valley

Despite their frequent use of the first-person singular, most spirituals are collective in meaning and were sung by a group. "That Lonesome Valley," however, seems highly individualistic. Perhaps based on the Twenty-third Psalm, it describes the fortitude necessary to meet the vicissitudes of life and death. These haunting lyrics lay bare the individual's need to face existence alone.

O, you got to walk-a that lonesome valley,
You got to go there by yourself;
No one here to go there with you,
You got to go there by yourself.

When you walk-a that lonesome valley,
You got to walk it by yourself;
No one here may walk it with you,
You got to walk it by yourself.

When you reach the River Jordan,
You got to cross it by yourself;
No one here may cross it with you,
You got to cross it by yourself.

When you face that judgment morning,
You got to face it by yourself;
No one here to face it for you,
You got to face it by yourself.

Loud and strong your Master calling,
You got to answer by yourself;
No one here to answer for you,
You got to answer by yourself.

You got to stand your trial in judgment,
You got to stand it by yourself;
No one here to stand it for you,
You got to stand it by yourself.

Jordan's stream is strong and chilly,
You got to wade it by yourself;
No one here to wade it for you,
You got to wade it by yourself.

When my dear Lord was hanging bleeding,
He had to hang there by His-self;
No one there could hang there for Him,
He had to hang there by His-self.

You got to join that Christian army,
You got to join it by yourself;
No one here to join it for you,
You got to join it by yourself.

You got to live a life of service,
You got to live it by yourself;
No one here to live it for you,
You got to live it by yourself.

The Welcome Table

SLAVES WERE FED JUST ENOUGH FOOD TO KEEP THEM PHYSICALLY ABLE *to work. At noontime a fellow slave would carry a bucket of cornmeal out to the fields and ladle a portion into each slave's outstretched hands. Little wonder that an image of the free North or Heaven was of a feast of milk and honey served to everyone gathered at the welcome table.*

I'm a-going to eat at the welcome table,
I'm a-going to eat at the welcome table,
Some of these days.

I'm a-going to feast on milk and honey,
I'm a-going to feast on milk and honey,
Some of these days.

I'm a-going to fly all around in Heaven,
I'm a-going to fly all around in Heaven,
Some of these days.

I'm a-going to wade across Jordan's river,
I'm a-going to wade across Jordan's river,
Some of these days.

Where Shall I Go?

FREDERICK DOUGLASS WROTE OF THE SPIRITUALS, "EVERY SONG WAS A *testimony against slavery, and a prayer and complaint boiling against slavery, and a prayer to God for deliverance from chains." "Where shall I go?" refers to the agonizing decision to liberate oneself by running away.*

Where shall I go?
Where shall I go?
Where shall I go
To ease my troubling mind?

I went to the rock to hide my face,
The rock cried out, "No hiding place."
The man who loves to serve the Lord
Will surely get his just reward.

Where shall I go?
Where shall I go?
Where shall I go
To ease my troubling mind?

Wish I Was in Heaven Sitting Down

THE SLAVES' IMAGE OF HEAVEN AS A PLACE TO SIT DOWN WITH "NOTHing to do" *is hardly surprising, given the constant tiring work demanded of them. The idealized vision here is of joining Mary and Martha sitting at Jesus' feet, as reported in John's gospel.*

Wish I was in Heaven sitting down,
Wish I was in Heaven sitting down,
O, Mary, O, Martha,
Wish I was in Heaven sitting down.

Wouldn't get tired no more, tired no more,
Wouldn't get tired no more, tired no more;
Wouldn't have nothing to do, nothing to do,
Wouldn't have nothing to do, nothing to do;

Try on my long white robe, long white robe,
Try on my long white robe, long white robe;
Sit at my Jesus' feet, my Jesus' feet,
Sit at my Jesus' feet, my Jesus' feet.

Wish I was in Heaven sitting down,
Wish I was in Heaven sitting down,
O, Mary, O, Martha,
Wish I was in Heaven sitting down.

You Got a Right

WHY IS THERE SO LITTLE HISTORICAL RECOGNITION OF THE SLAVES' *resistance to and revolt against bondage? Arthur Schomburg (1874–1938), the African-American intellectual and book collector, claimed that one of the secrets of black history is that black people played a major role in their own liberation. Emancipation was not a gift of benevolent whites, but the result of 250 years of struggle by men and women who never gave up believing "We all got a right to the tree of life."*

You got a right, I got a right,
We all got a right to the tree of life.
Yes, tree of life.

The very time I thought I was lost,
The dungeon shook and the chain fell off.
You may hinder me here,
But you can't hinder me there.
'Cause God in the Heaven's
Going to answer my prayer.

O, brother, O, sister,
You got a right, I got a right,
We all got a right to the tree of life.
Yes, tree of life.

Many Thousand Gone

PERHAPS NO SPIRITUAL SPEAKS MORE DIRECTLY TO THE SLAVE EXPERI-
*ence than "Many Thousand Gone" because it does not even attempt to hide or code
its meaning. The lyrics describe what the thousands of runaway slaves had escaped:
being sold like animals, short rations, the physical torture of the whip. John Lovell,
Jr., one of the leading scholars of the spirituals, says that "no more passionate songs
have ever been written to proclaim the concept of freedom," and he particularly cites
this spiritual's cry of protest: "No more, no more."*

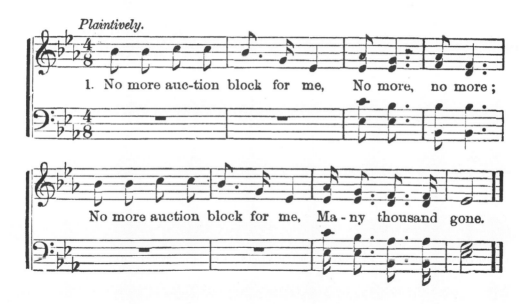

No more peck o' corn for me . . .

No more driver's lash for me . . .

No more pint o' salt for me . . .

No more hundred lash for me . . .

No more mistress's call for me . . .

Songs of
hope

The Gospel Train

THIS SPIRITUAL MAY BE ADAPTED FROM A WHITE HYMN, BUT THE SLAVE *poet has creatively used everyday images as symbols of liberation. As already noted, the train is always a metaphor for escape. The gospel train is fully egalitarian ("no second class on board") and integrates the Hebrew Bible and the New Testament ("There's Moses, Noah, and . . . our friends in Christ").*

1. The gos-pel train is com-ing, I hear it just at
2. I hear the bell and whis-tle, The com-ing round the
3. No sig-nal for an-oth-er train To fol-low on the

hand, I hear the car wheels moving, And rumbling thro' the land.
curve; She's playing all her steam and pow'r And straining every nerve.
line, O, sinner, you're forever lost, If once you're left be-hind.

Get on board, chil-dren, Get on board, chil-dren, Get on

board, children, For there's room for ma-ny a more. more.

This is the Christian banner,
　The motto's new and old,
Salvation and repentance
　Are burnished there in gold.
Chorus: Get on board, children . . .

She's nearing now the station,
　O, sinner, don't be vain,
But come and get your ticket,
　And be ready for the train.
Chorus: Get on board, children . . .

The fare is cheap and all can go,
　The rich and poor are there,
No second class on board the train,
　No difference in the fare.
Chorus: Get on board, children . . .

There's Moses, Noah, and Abraham,
　And all the prophets, too,
Our friends in Christ are all on board,
　O, what a heavenly crew.
Chorus: Get on board, children . . .

We soon shall reach the station,
　O, how we then shall sing,
With all the heavenly army,
　We'll make the welcome ring,
Chorus: Get on board, children . . .

We'll shout o'or all our sorrows,
　And sing forever more,
With Christ and all His army,
　On that celestial shore.
Chorus: Get on board, children . . .

Am I Born to Die?

PERHAPS ADAPTED FROM AN EVANGELICAL HYMN, THIS SPIRITUAL POINTS *as directly as an arrow to the question at the center of human life. As a Christian, the slave poet is struck by the sacrificial purpose of Jesus' life and death. The question Jesus asks was all too familiar to those trapped in the slave system, which caused a great many black men, women, and children to "lay this body down." Do their deaths have meaning? It is the implicit hope of this song that they do.*

Dark was the night and cold the ground
On which the Lord was laid:
His sweat like drops of blood ran down,
In agony He prayed
Am I born to die,
Am I born to die,
Am I born to die,
To lay this body down?

Father, remove this bitter cup,
If such Thy sacred will;
If not, content to drink it up
Thy pleasure to fulfill.

Go to the garden, sinner, see
Those precious drops there flow,
The heavy load He bore for thee,
For there He lie so low.

Then leave of Him the cross to bear
Thy Father's will obey,
And when temptations press thee near
Awake, to watch and pray.

Am I born to die,
Am I born to die,
Am I born to die,
Am I born to die?

The Angels Are Watching Over Me

ALAIN LOCKE, THE FIRST AFRICAN-AMERICAN RHODES SCHOLAR AND A
*professor of philosophy at Howard University, wrote that the spirituals "rank
among the classic folk expressions in the whole world because of their moving simplicity, their characteristic originality, and their universal appeal." The slaves' profound sense of hopefulness is demonstrated in these lyrics with their insistence that
"the angels are watching over me."*

All night, all night,
The angels are watching over me.
All night, all night,
The angels are watching over me.

Someday Peter and someday Paul,
The angels are watching over me—
Ain't but one God made us all,
The angels are watching over me.

You get there before I do,
The angels are watching over me—
Tell all my friends I'm coming too.
The angels are watching over me.

Babylon's Falling

THE SLAVES DID NOT LET GO OF THEIR HOPE FOR THE DESTRUCTION OF *Babylon, a familiar biblical image for the wicked and corrupt world. A righteous God can be depended upon ultimately to destroy sin, particularly what Methodist founder John Wesley called "the sum of all evils": human slavery and the economic and political system that supported it. There are echoes of this spiritual in the songs of Bob Marley and other Rastafarians who continue to see this world as Babylon.*

Pure city, Babylon's falling, to rise no more,
Pure city, Babylon's falling, to rise no more.
O, Babylon's falling, falling, falling,
Babylon's falling to rise no more,
O, Babylon's falling, falling, falling,
Babylon's falling to rise no more.

O, Jesus told you once before,
Babylon's falling to rise no more;
To go in peace and sin no more,
Babylon's falling to rise no more.

If you get there before I do,
Babylon's falling to rise no more;
Tell all my friends I'm coming too,
Babylon's falling to rise no more.

Balm in Gilead

ONE OF THE MOST BEAUTIFUL OF ALL THE SPIRITUALS, "BALM IN *Gilead" answers a question asked by the prophet Jeremiah: "Is there no balm in Gilead? Is there no physician there?" Jeremiah's plaintive query arose from the adversities faced by Israel: "Listen to the cry of my people from a land far away. Why then is there no healing for the wounds of my people?" African-American slaves identified with Jeremiah's circumstances and with his question. Surprisingly, perhaps, their answer is hopeful and affirmative.*

There is a balm in Gilead
To make the wounded whole,
There is a balm in Gilead
To heal the sin-sick soul.

Sometimes I feel discouraged
And think my work's in vain,
But then the Holy Spirit
Revives my soul again.

Don't ever feel discouraged,
For Jesus is your friend,
And if you lack for knowledge,
He'll never refuse to lend.

If you cannot sing like angels,
If you cannot preach like Paul,
You can tell the love of Jesus,
And say, "He died for all."

Be with Me

Novelist and Nobel laureate Toni Morrison says there is a *national amnesia about slavery, that it is the unspeakable part of American history. In her fiction, perhaps most vividly in* Beloved, *she makes readers remember what American society and culture try to make us forget. Spirituals are, in a sense, historical documents, recalling some of that lost history by giving us a glimpse into slaves' hearts and minds and thus into their unwritten experiences. This song provides just such a glimpse.*

Be with me, Lord! Be with me!
Be with me, Lord! Be with me!

When I'm in trouble, be with me!
When I'm in trouble, be with me!

When I'm dying, be with me!
When I'm dying, be with me!

When I'm on my lonesome journey,
I want Jesus to be with me.

Before This Time Another Year

AT ONE LEVEL, THIS SPIRITUAL IS ABOUT DEATH; "BROKE THE ICE" IS AN *unexpected and colorful metaphor. The repeated cry "how long?" suggests a longing to end the suffering caused by slavery. And slaves yearned for reunion with family and ancestors in Africa after death. Yet we know African Americans never gave up hope, so we can be sure "I may be gone" is also a coded message about escape.*

Before this time another year I may be gone,
Out in some lonely graveyard,
O, Lord, how long?

My mother's broke the ice and gone,
O, Lord, how long?
By the grace of God I'll follow on,
O, Lord, how long?

My father's broke the ice and gone,
O, Lord, how long?
By the grace of God I'll follow on,
O, Lord, how long?

My Savior's broke the ice and gone,
O, Lord, how long?
By the grace of God I'll follow on,
O, Lord, how long?

The Book of Life

THE TERM *SPIRITUAL* PROBABLY COMES FROM THE POPULAR EVANGELICAL *camp meetings that flourished in Kentucky and elsewhere on the early frontier. Blacks and whites who participated sang not only the standard church hymns, but also more informal tunes called "spiritual songs," which were religious in nature, but not quite hymns. The African Americans' own unique songs more closely resembled "spiritual songs" than they did hymns.*

Brother Joe, you ought to know my name,
Hallelujah,
My name is written in the book of life;
If you look in the book you'll find it there.

One morning I was a-walking down,
I saw the berry hanging down, Lord,
I picked the berry and I sucked the juice,

Just as sweet as the honey in the comb,
I wonder when father Jimmy's gone,
My father's gone to the yonder world.

You dig the spring that's never dry,
The more I dig, the water springs,
The water springs that's never dry.

By and By

IN THESE BITTERSWEET LYRICS THE SLAVE POET—SEPARATED FROM HIS *or her nation, community, and family—calls out in hope: "By and by we shall all meet again." But these words are followed by a moving and arresting phrase, "And I wouldn't mind dying if dying was all."*

By and by we all shall meet again,
By and by we all shall meet again,
O, by and by, we all shall meet again,
And I wouldn't mind dying if dying was all.

After death got to fill an empty grave,
After death got to fill an empty grave,
After death got to fill an empty grave,
And I wouldn't mind dying if dying was all.

Come Trembling Down

THE IDEAS, CONCEPTS, AND ACTUAL TEXTS OF MANY SPIRITUALS *undoubtedly originated in felicitous phrases of slave preachers' extemporaneous sermons. In addition, black preaching—with its melodious, rhythmic cadence (called "chanting" by some) and antiphonal responses from the congregation—can be seen as a model for the structure of spirituals.*

Come trembling down, go shouting home,
Safe in the sweet arms of Jesus,
Come Jesus;
'Twas just about the break of day,
King Jesus stole my heart away.

Come trembling down, go shouting home,
Safe in the sweet arms of Jesus,
Come Jesus.

The Angels Done Changed My Name

DENIED ANY WAY, EXCEPT ESCAPE, OF IMPROVING THEIR PLIGHT, THE *slaves lived on hope. Acceptance by God offered the possibility of a new identity, with a new name. The slaves were not allowed to use their African names; they were usually given only a first name by the slave masters, who often chose an animal's name or a supposedly humorous name. So a new name was essential for the "coming day," a day when all things would be made new and God would proclaim the slaves' human status and set them free.*

1. I went to the hill side, I went to pray, I
2. I looked at my hands and my hands were new, I

know the an - gels done changed my name, Done
know the an - gels done changed my name, I

changed my name for the com - ing day, Thank
looked at my feet and my feet were too, Thank

CHORUS.

God the angels done changed my name. } Done
God the angels done changed my name. }

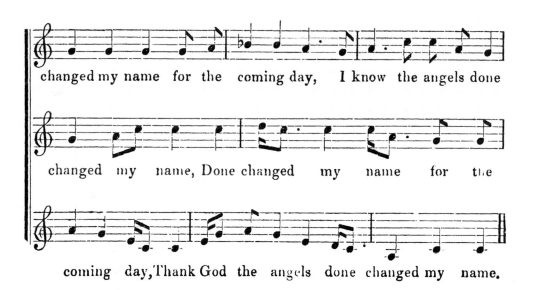

changed my name for the coming day, I know the angels done

changed my name, Done changed my name for the

coming day, Thank God the angels done changed my name.

Don't Get Weary

SOLOMON NORTHUP, THE RUNAWAY WHO WROTE *TWELVE YEARS A Slave*, *said that those in bondage maintained secret thoughts never expressed in front of white people, that they fully comprehended their situation and yearned for freedom as passionately as all other people. This spiritual encourages African Americans not to lose heart in the freedom struggle.*

Members, don't get weary,
Members, don't get weary,
Members, don't get weary,
For the work's almost done.

O, keep your lamps trimmed and a-burning,
Keep your lamps trimmed and a-burning,
Keep your lamps trimmed and a-burning,
For the work's almost done.

Don't Leave Me, Lord

THE RHYTHM FOR THE SPIRITUALS WAS OFTEN ACCENTUATED BY CARRY-*overs from African dancing: enthusiastic singers clapped their hands, slapped their thighs, stamped their feet, shook their heads, and swayed their bodies. As historian Albert Raboteau, author of* Slave Religion, *points out, this communal movement was a dramatization of the songs. At times the singing was accompanied by the ring shout, a group circle movement, technically not dancing, which often built to religious ecstasy. This spiritual lends itself to that rhythm.*

Don't leave me, Lord,
Don't leave me, Lord,
Lord, don't leave me behind;
Don't leave me, Lord,
Don't leave me, Lord,
Lord, don't leave me behind.

Jesus, Jesus is my friend,
He will go with me to the end;
No use talking about what you going to do,
Don't tend to deny my God for you;
I don't want to stumble,
And I don't want to stop,
I don't want to be no stumbling block.

Don't leave me, Lord,
Don't leave me, Lord,
Lord, don't leave me behind.

Dry Bones

IN THE STORY TOLD IN THE HEBREW BIBLE GOD TAKES EZEKIEL TO A *valley full of dry bones and bids him prophesy that God can and will bring them back to life. Ezekiel does so, and the rattling bones begin to come together, bone to bone. This is a metaphor, God explains, for his people, who are spiritually dead, who have lost hope, and who have become, as one translation has it, "severed off to ourselves." For African-American slaves, it was as if God were speaking directly to them: "I will put my spirit into you, and you shall live, and I will return you to your own land" (Ezekiel 37:14).*

God called Ezekiel by His word,
"Go down and prophesy!"
"Yes, Lord!"
Ezekiel prophesied by the power of God,
Commanded the bones to rise.

They gonna walk around, dry bones,
They gonna walk around, with the dry
    bones,
They gonna walk around, dry bones,
Why don't you rise and hear the word of the
    Lord?
"Tell me, how did the bones get together
    with the long bones? Prophesy?"

Ah, well, the toe bone connected with the
    foot bone,
The foot bone connected with the ankle
    bone,
The ankle bone connected with the leg
    bone,
The leg bone connected with the knee bone,
The knee bone connected with the thigh
    bone,
Rise and hear the word of the Lord!

Early in the Morning

ACCORDING TO MUSIC HISTORIAN DENA J. EPSTEIN, THE "EARLIEST
*known mention of distinctive black religious music" was in 1819, when John F.
Watson, a white Methodist, criticized African-American participants in evangelis-
tic camp meetings for their body movements, repetitive choruses, and "merry airs."
These are characteristics of African music unfamiliar to European Americans.*

I met little Rosa early in the morning,
And I asked her,
How're you doing, my daughter?

O, Jerusalem, early in the morning,
Walk 'em easy around the Heaven,
Walk 'em easy around the Heaven,
O, Jerusalem, early in the morning,
Walk 'em easy around the Heaven,
Till all living may join that band.

Going to Shout All Over God's Heaven

THE SLAVES' PICTURE OF LIFE IN HEAVEN OR IN A FREE LAND OFFERS *contrasts to the hard realities of life in chains. Instead of the lowest grade of coarse cloth, everybody will have a robe. Instead of bare feet, even during the winter, everybody will have shoes. Instead of the silence imposed by servitude, everybody will shout a "new song." But only God's children will enjoy this new life. In a direct jab at churchgoing slave owners, the slave poet declares: "Everybody talking about Heaven ain't going there."*

I've got a robe, you've got a robe,
All of God's children got a robe;
When I get to Heaven,
Going to put on my robe,
Going to shout all over God's Heaven.
Heaven, Heaven,
Everybody talking about Heaven ain't going
    there.

I've got a crown, you've got a crown,
All of God's children got a crown;
When I get to Heaven,
Going to put on my crown,
Going to shout all over God's Heaven.
Heaven, Heaven,
Everybody talking about Heaven ain't going
    there.

I've got shoes, you've got shoes,
All of God's children got shoes;
When I get to Heaven,
Going to put on my shoes,

Going to walk all over God's Heaven.
Heaven, Heaven,
Everybody talking about Heaven ain't going
    there.

I've got a harp, you've got a harp,
All of God's children got a harp;
When I get to Heaven,
Going to play all over God's Heaven.
Heaven, Heaven,
Everybody talking about Heaven ain't going
    there.

I've got a song, you've got a song,
All of God's children got a song;
When I get to Heaven,
Going to sing my new song,
Going to sing all over God's Heaven.
Heaven, Heaven,
Everybody talking about Heaven ain't going
    there;
Going to shout all over God's Heaven.

Good Lord, Shall I Ever Be the One?

Historian Albert Raboteau claims, "It was in the spirituals above all that the characters, themes, and lessons of the Bible became dramatically real and took on special meaning for the slaves." They could identify with Adam, who disobeyed his Lord, who tried to escape, and who finally responded in hopeful faith. And they could dream of freedom: "Shall I ever be the one to get over in the Promised Land?"

Good Lord, shall I ever be the one?
Good Lord, shall I ever be the one?
Good Lord, shall I ever be the one,
To get over in the Promised Land?

God placed Adam in the garden,
'Twas about the cool of the day,
Called for old Adam,
And he tried to run away.

The Lord walked in the garden,
'Twas about the cool of the day,
Called for old Adam,
And Adam said, "Hear me, Lord."

Good Lord, shall I ever be the one?
Good Lord, shall I ever be the one?
Good Lord, shall I ever be the one,
To get over in the Promised Land?

Good-bye, Brothers

THIS MAY BE A PARTING HYMN AT THE CONCLUSION OF A RELIGIOUS SER-
*vice; it may be the good-bye of someone planning to escape; it may be a dying
Christian's farewell. Most likely, however, it was sung when the owners sold off one
of a slave's family members and thereby broke, usually forever, the closest ties of
human kinship. What could the members of a family about to be destroyed say to
each other but the hopeful words "We'll part in the body, we'll meet in the spirit"?*

Good-bye, brothers, good-bye, sisters,
If I don't see you anymore;
I'll meet you in Heaven
In the blessed kingdom,
If I don't see you anymore.
We'll part in the body,

We'll meet in the spirit,
If I don't see you anymore;
So now God bless you,
God bless you,
If I don't see you anymore.

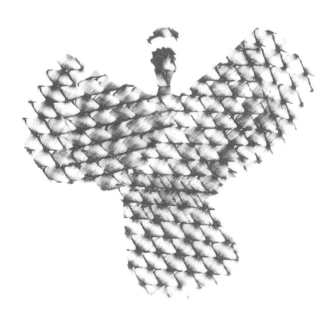

My Lord, What a Mourning

THE TITLE OF THIS SPIRITUAL IS AMBIGUOUS. IN SOME VERSIONS THE *word is* mourning, *in others, it's* morning. *Judith Fleischer, a scholar who has written about slave narratives, says, "Slave lives were filled with mournings after mournings; and denied direct expression of this grief, they, like other people, would find it in other ways." When the text is read with the word* morning, *however, the song is an extraordinary affirmation of hope, for God himself will "wake the nations."*

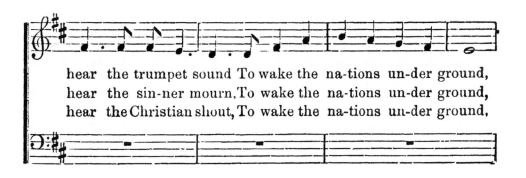

hear the trumpet sound To wake the na-tions un-der ground,
hear the sin-ner mourn, To wake the na-tions un-der ground,
hear the Christian shout, To wake the na-tions un-der ground,

Looking to my God's right hand, When the stars begin to fall.

The Graveyard

THE SPIRITUALS BECAME WIDELY KNOWN AND PRESERVED BECAUSE OF *the Fisk Jubilee Singers. Fisk University was established in Nashville, Tennessee, to serve the freedpeople who yearned to read and write. Students sold the iron chains from the city's slave pens to buy spelling books. To raise funds, Professor George L. White organized a group of student singers, who set out on October 6, 1871, to tour the Northeast. They met with little success singing white music, but when they sang spirituals like this one their audiences were electrified.*

Who's going to lay this body, member?
O, shout glory,
And who's going to lay this body?
O, ring Jerusalem.

O, call all the members to the graveyard,
O, graveyard ought to know me,
O, grass grow in the graveyard,
O, I reel and I rock in the graveyard,
O, I walk and toss with Jesus,
My mother reel and toss with the fever,

I have a grandmother in the graveyard,
O, where do you think I find them?
I find them, Lord, in the graveyard,
I reel, and I rock, and I'm going home,
O, repeat that story over.

Graveyard, you ought to know me,
Who's going to lay this body, member?
O, shout glory,
And who's going to lay this body?
O, ring Jerusalem.

Hard Trials

THROUGH HARD TIMES AND TRIBULATIONS, ALL GOD'S CHILDREN HAVE found a true hiding place: "I'm going to live with God."

The foxes have holes in the ground,
The birds have nests in the air,
The Christians have a hiding place,
But we poor sinners have none.
Now ain't them hard trials, tribulations?
Ain't them hard trials?
I'm going to live with God!

Old Satan tempted Eve,
And Eve, she tempted Adam;
And that's why the sinner has to pray so
    hard
To get his sins forgiven.

Oh, Methodist, Methodist is my name,
Methodist till I die;
I'll be baptized on the Methodist side,
and a Methodist will I die.

Oh, Baptist, Baptist is my name,
Baptist till I die;
I'll be baptized on the Baptist side,
And a Baptist will I die.

While marching on the road,
A-hunting for a home,
You had better stop your differences
And travel on to God.

The foxes have holes in the ground,
The birds have nests in the air,
The Christians have a hiding place,
But we poor sinners have none.
Now ain't them hard trials, tribulations?
Ain't them hard trials?
I'm going to live with God!

I Ain't Going to Grief My Lord No More

WITH THE VERBAL ART OF THE AFRICAN ORAL TRADITION, THE SLAVES *retold in verse and song the Bible stories they heard in the evangelical Protestant culture. When linked together, these spirituals recount the biblical images, personalities, and stories that resonated with the slaves in their own lives. As historian Albert Raboteau writes, "Themes and events from the Old and New Testaments were used by the slaves to interpret their own experience by measuring it against a wider system of meaning."*

I ain't going to grief my Lord no more
For the Bible tell me so,
I ain't going to grief my Lord no more.

The tallest tree in paradise,
The Christians call the tree of life;
I ain't going to grief my Lord no more
For the Bible tell me so.

O, Paul and Silas bound in jail,
The one did sing while the other prayed.

I wants to go to Heaven and I wants to go
   right,
I wants to go to Heaven all dressed in white.

O, look up yonder what I see,
Bright angels coming after me.

If you get there before I do,
Look out for me, I'm coming, too.

O, my name done written, done written
   down fine,
O, my name done written, in David's line.

How Long?

IT HAS BEEN SUGGESTED THAT AFRICAN-AMERICAN CULTURE BEGAN ON *the upper decks of the slave ships during the painful Middle Passage between Africa and the New World. There the slaves were forced under the whips and lashes of the ship's crew to improvise dances for exercise. Whatever singing took place was in African languages, as were the earliest versions of what we now know as the spirituals. The original texts of the first spirituals were never written down and are lost forever.*

When the clouds hang heavy and it looks
    like rain,
O Lord, how long?
Well, the sun's drawing water from every
    vein,
O Lord, how long?

About this time another year,
I may be gone,
Within some lonely graveyard—
O Lord, how long?

If I had prayed when I was young,
O Lord, how long?
Well, I would not've had such a hard race to
    run.
O Lord, how long?

I Can't Stay Away

IN *RE-SEARCHING BLACK MUSIC*, JON MICHAEL SPENCER WRITES, "THE *African rhythms of black preaching comprise the single ingredient that gives the melodiousness of traditional black sermonry both its momentum and its momentousness."* One can hear those rhythms in the phrases of this spiritual.

Moaner, why don't you pray?
Moaner, why don't you pray?
Moaner, why don't you pray?
I can't stay away.

Give-a my life to live with Jesus,
Give-a my life to live with Jesus,
Give-a my life to live with Jesus,
I can't stay away.

I'm going home to live with Jesus,
Long white robe in the Heaven for me,
Golden girdle in the Heaven for me,
Golden slippers in the Heaven for me,
Starry crown in the Heaven for me,
I can't stay away.

I Have Another Building

THE SPIRITUALS ARE ALIVE WITH TROPES AND METAPHORS, PARTLY THE
*genius of the unknown slave poets, partly the secret language that transmitted coded
messages throughout the slave community. Canaan was Canada, home was Africa,
the Jordan was the first step to freedom, Babylon was the slavocracy, Hell was the
Deep South, King Jesus was the slaves' protector and benefactor. A building not
made with hands is a New Testament metaphor for God's kingdom. Here it implies
dwelling in freedom, freedom as a state of mind as well as one of the free states of
the Union.*

I know I have another building,
I know it's not made with hands,
   O brethren;
I want to go to Heaven and I want to go
   right,
O, I want to go to Heaven all robed in white.

I haven't been to Heaven but I've been told,
O, the gates are pearl and the streets are
   gold;
I look over yonder and what do I see?
A band of angels coming after me.

I know I have another building,
I know I have another building,
I know it's not made with hands.

I'm Going Where There Ain't No More Dying

THIS SPIRITUAL IS A VARIATION OF "JOSHUA FIT THE BATTLE OF *Jericho." Joshua's battle was a popular theme in slave songs and preaching, because it was seen as a symbol of God's freeing the weak and powerless from their oppressors, and liberating the lowly and downtrodden from the proud and mighty.*

Joshua fought the battle 'round Jericho's
    wall,
I'm going where there ain't no more dying;
And he kicked a brick out of Satan's hall,
I'm going where there ain't no more dying;
Children, A-amen,
Children, A-amen,
I'm going where there ain't no more dying.

And the second time around the sun stopped
    sitting,
The sun stopped sitting down;
The third time around the children were
    a-blowing,
The children were a-blowing strong;
The fourth time around the wall came
    a-tumbling,
The wall came a-tumbling down.

Children, A-amen,
Children, A-amen,
I'm going where there ain't no more dying.

In That Great Getting-up Morning

IN *THE SOULS OF BLACK FOLK*, W. E. B. DU BOIS, THE GREATEST
*African-American intellectual of his time, wrote of the spirituals: "Through all the
sorrow songs there breathes a hope, a faith in the ultimate justice of things." This
song, for example, promises "a better day a-coming," when "you'll see the righteous marching." That this would be a time not only of justice but also of retribution
is implied by the image of "the world on fire."*

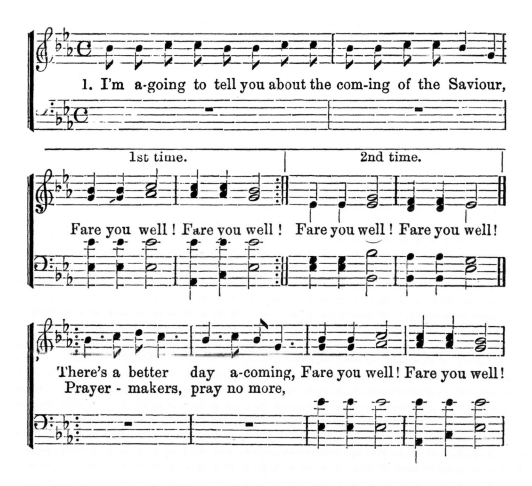

1. I'm a-going to tell you about the com-ing of the Saviour,

1st time. 2nd time.

Fare you well! Fare you well! Fare you well! Fare you well!

There's a better day a-coming, Fare you well! Fare you well!
Prayer - makers, pray no more,

Oh, preachers, fold your Bibles, Fare you well! Fare you well!
For the last soul's con-vert-ed,

In that great getting-up morning, Fare you well! Fare you well!

In that great getting-up morning, Fare you well! Fare you well!

The Lord spoke to Gabriel:
"Go look behind the altar,
Take down the silver trumpet,
Blow your trumpet, Gabriel."
"Lord, how loud shall I blow it?"
"Blow it right calm and easy,
Do not alarm My people,
Tell them to come to judgment;
Gabriel, blow your trumpet."
"Lord, how loud shall I blow it?"
"Loud as seven peals of thunder!
Wake the sleeping nations."

Then you'll see poor sinners rising;
Then you'll see the world on fire;
See the moon a-bleeding,
See the stars falling,
See the elements melting,
See the forked lightning,
Hear the rumbling thunder;
Earth shall reel and totter.
Then you'll see the Christians rising;
Then you'll see the righteous marching,
See them marching home to Heaven.
Then you'll see my Jesus coming
With all His holy angels,
Take the righteous home to Heaven,
There they'll live with God forever.

General Roll Call

THE SLAVE SYSTEM MADE THE PLANTATION SOUTH INTO A VAST PRISON, *where the slaves were constantly watched and there were regular head counts. A roll call was thus a familiar occurrence. In this spiritual the slave poet uses the roll call to signify that men and women will be present and ready—either for a new life in Heaven or for God's dispensation of freedom on earth.*

O come, my brethren, one and all,
When the general roll is called I'll be there;
O let's get ready when Gabriel calls,
When the general roll is called I'll be there.

I'll be there, I'll be there, I'll be there,
I'll be there,
When the general roll is called I'll be there.

Inching Along

The lowly inchworm may seem an inappropriate image for a spiritual, *but it demonstrates the slave poets' creative use of their immediate environment for religious metaphors. Perhaps this particular image began as an illustration in a sermon by a black preacher. The earthly message is one of encouragement to keep going against the odds. There is a hopeful affirmation that, slowly but surely, we'll "get home."*

Keep a-inching along,
Keep a-inching along;
Jesus will come by and by;
Keep a-inching along
Like a poor inchworm,
Jesus will come by and by.

'Twas inch by inch
I sought the Lord;
And inch by inch
He blessed my soul;
The Lord is coming to take us home,

And then our work will soon be done;
Trials and troubles are on the way,
But we must watch and always pray;
We'll inch and inch along,
And inch and inch till we get home.

Keep a-inching along,
Keep a-inching along;
Jesus will come by and by;
Keep a-inching along,
Like a poor inchworm,
Jesus will come by and by.

I've Got a Mother in the Heavens

This song has multiple layers of meaning. It promises life in Heaven beyond life on earth. It speaks of family members who have escaped from slavery and who are free, perhaps in the North or Canada. Yet it also recalls mothers, fathers, and sisters wrenched apart at the auction block for the slave owner's financial gain. Still, this is primarily a song of hope: "We will outshine the sun."

I've got a mother in the heavens,
Outshines the sun,
Outshines the sun, outshines the sun,
I've got a mother in the heavens,
Outshines the sun,
Way beyond the moon.

I've got a father in the heavens,
Outshines the sun,
Outshines the sun, outshines the sun,
I've got a father in the heavens,
Outshines the sun,
Way beyond the moon.

I've got a sister in the heavens,
Outshines the sun,
Outshines the sun, outshines the sun,
I've got a sister in the heavens,
Outshines the sun,
Way beyond the moon.

When we get to Heaven,
We will outshine the sun,
Outshine the sun, outshine the sun,
When we get to Heaven,
We will outshine the sun,
Way beyond the moon.

I Want to See Jesus in the Morning

THIS SONG SHOWS THE SPIRITUALS' STRUCTURAL CONNECTION TO African-American preaching. The list of "I wants" is more an oratorical device than a musical or even poetic one. Jon Michael Spencer, an astute commentator on black music, writes, "Even contemporary black preachers who have drawn artistically from the experience of having heard black music at its authentic source continue to pursue the skill of improvisationally fitting the phrases and sentences together into quasi-metrical units."

In the morning,
O, in the morning,
I want to see Jesus in the morning.

I want to see my Jesus at the breaking of the
day,
I want to see my Jesus at the rising of the
sun;
I want to see my Jesus in the morning,
I want to see my Jesus when the sinner man
runs;
I want to see my Jesus in the morning.

I want to see my Jesus when the tombstone's
busted,
I want to see my Jesus in the morning;
I want to see my Jesus when this world's on
fire,
I want to see my Jesus in the morning.

I want to see my Jesus when the dead be
rising,
I want to see my Jesus in the morning.

Jacob's Ladder

THIS SPIRITUAL HAS RETAINED ITS POPULARITY OVER THE YEARS. It *draws on the biblical image of Jacob's ladder as a metaphor for advancement, and invokes the courage and fortitude of the dedicated soldier. Perhaps the most interesting aspect of the song, however, is its question "If you love Him, why not serve Him?" John Lovell, Jr., comments, "This method is obviously more than call and response. It presumes that the listener is part of the song. What he thinks and feels, how he reacts to the whole big event, are part of the story. This utter involvement is invigorating to singer and listeners."*

We are climbing Jacob's ladder,
We are climbing Jacob's ladder,
We are climbing Jacob's ladder,
Soldier of the cross.

Every round goes higher and higher,
Soldier of the cross.

Sinner, do you love my Jesus?
Soldier of the cross.
If you love Him, why not serve Him?
Soldier of the cross.

Do you think I'd make a soldier?
Soldier of the cross.

We are climbing higher and higher,
Soldier of the cross.

Jesus on the Waterside

TOWARD THE END OF THE NINETEENTH CENTURY, SPIRITUALS, WHICH *were a local manifestation of African-American culture, became an international musical phenomenon. Colin Brown, a music critic in Glasgow, Scotland, wrote of the touring Fisk Jubilee Singers, "As to the manner of their singing, it must be heard before it can be realized. . . . It gives a new musical idea." This spiritual reveals the unique poetic style of the slave songs.*

Heaven's bell a-ringing,
I know the road;
Heaven's bell a-ringing,
I know the road;
Heaven's bell a-ringing,
I know the road,
Jesus is sitting on the waterside.

Do come along,
Do let us go,
Do come along,
Do let us go,
Do come along,
Do let us go,
Jesus is sitting on the waterside.

Just Like John

THESE LYRICS PROCLAIM THAT WHEN "THE WORLD'S ON FIRE" AND THE *present wicked social order comes to an end, slaves will find freedom in the next world if not in this one. They will have the freedom to "walk Jerusalem just like John." It was "to these songs," Frederick Douglass wrote in his autobiography, "I trace my first glimmering of the dehumanizing character of slavery."*

When I come to die,
I want to be ready,
When I come to die,
Going to walk Jerusalem just like John.

Walk Jerusalem in the morning,
I'm going to walk Jerusalem in the
    morning;
Walk Jerusalem when the world's on fire,

I'm going to walk Jerusalem just like John;
Walk Jerusalem when the tombstone's
    busted,
Walk Jerusalem just like John.

When I come to die,
I want to be ready,
When I come to die,
Going to walk Jerusalem just like John.

Lay This Body Down

THIS IS ONE OF THE FIRST SPIRITUALS TO BE HEARD AND WRITTEN DOWN *by a sympathetic white listener. Of the line "I'll lay in the grave and stretch out my arms," Thomas Wentworth Higginson, a radical abolitionist, confidant of Emily Dickinson, and a Union officer commanding African-American troops in the Civil War, said: "[N]ever, it seems to me, since man first lived and suffered, was his infinite longing for peace uttered more plaintively than in that line."*

I know moonlight, I know starlight;
I lay this body down.
I walk in the graveyard, I walk through the
    graveyard
To lay this body down.
I lay in the grave and stretch out my arms;
I lay this body down.

I go to the judgment in the evening of the
    day
When I lay this body down.
And my soul and your soul will meet in the
    day
When we lay our bodies down.

May Be the Last Time

WILLIAM SINCLAIR, AN ESCAPED SLAVE, REPORTED THAT MASTERS *often forbade the singing of spirituals that they suspected might be about freedom. When that happened, Sinclair says, the slaves merely hummed the music "while the words echoed and re-echoed deep down in their hearts with perhaps greater effect than if they had been spoken."*

I don't know, I don't know, I don't know;
May be the last time, I don't know,
I don't know.

May be the last time you'll hear me pray,
May be the last time, I don't know;
May be the last time you'll hear me pray,
May be the last time, I don't know.

I don't know, I don't know, I don't know;
May be the last time, I don't know,
I don't know.

Old Ship of Zion

THE "OLD SHIP OF ZION" IS GENERALLY CONSIDERED AN AFRICAN-
*American metaphor for the black church. But there are various layers and levels of
meaning here. Many slaves were sailors and boatmen, both along the coast and on
inland waterways. Also, in African cosmologies a river might be the way to the next
world. In this world the "Old Ship of Zion" might even be transport back to Africa.
As the theologian James Cone writes, "In the spirituals, black slaves combined a
memory of their fathers with the Christian gospel and created a style of existence
that participated in their liberation from earthly bondage."*

In singing the last two verses the music is not to be repeated.

She has landed many a thousand. Hallelujah.
She has landed many a thousand. Hallelu.
She has landed many a thousand,
And will land as many a more. O glory,
   Hallelu.

She is loaded down with angels. Hallelujah.
She is loaded down with angels. Hallelu.
And King Jesus is the captain,
And He'll carry us all home. O glory,
   Hallelu.

Move Along

WITH THEIR MORE SENTIMENTAL LANGUAGE, THESE LYRICS SOUND AS IF *they might have been adapted from an evangelical hymn. Their vision is a hopeful one: "Move along," they urge, "to the heavenly home." The reference to Africa, across the ocean, is clear. As V. F. Calverton points out in his 1940 essay "The Negro and American Culture," the spirituals are religious hymns but they also "constitute the aching, poignant cries of an enslaved people separated from their homeland."*

Let us move along, move along,
Move along to the heavenly home,
Let us move along, move along,
I am bound to meet you there.

We are on the ocean sailing,
And awhile must face the stormy blast,
But if Jesus is our captain,
We will make the port at last.

Yonder see the golden city,
And the lighthouse gleaming on the shore,
Hear the angels sweetly singing,
Soon our journey will be o'er.

There we'll meet our friends in Jesus,
Who are waiting on the golden shore,
With a shout of joy they'll greet us,
When we meet to part no more.

Let us move along, move along,
Move along to the heavenly home,
Let us move along, move along,
I am bound to meet you there.

O Lord, Write My Name

THE 1860 EDITION OF THE CODE OF VIRGINIA CALLED FOR THE WHIP-*ping of any slaves who were taught to read or write. Another punishment for a slave caught reading was to have his right forefinger cut off. To sing, "O Lord, write my name," therefore, meant not only to be listed in the divine Book of Life but to defy the law of the state. Also, to have one's name written down is to participate in the mystery of words and the power of naming.*

O Lord, write my name;
O Lord, write my name;
O Lord, write my name;
The angel in Heaven going to write my
　name.

Better mind, sister, how you walk on the
　cross;
If your right foot slip,
Your soul will be lost.
Come on brother, with your up and down;
Christ going to meet you on the halfway
　ground.

Joshua was the son of Nun;
God was with him till the work was done.
God in the garden and began to look out;
The ram horn blow and the children did
　shout.

O Lord, write my name;
O Lord, write my name;
O Lord, write my name;
The angel in Heaven going to write my
　name.

Then My Little Soul's Going to Shine

THE SPIRITUALS ARE BOTH INDIVIDUALISTIC AND COLLECTIVE. THE *singer here is going to climb Jacob's ladder and sit at the welcome table, but he or she is going to do so as part of "the great association," that is, as part of the whole community of free and redeemed African Americans. This world is transcended, but it is not entirely forgotten: while feasting on milk and honey, the singer vows "to tell God how-a you starved me," reporting a still-remembered human injustice to a just and retributive God. But the overwhelming theme is hopeful: "Then my little soul's going to shine."*

I'm going to join the great association,
I'm going to join the great association,
I'm going to join the great association,
Then my little soul's going to shine, shine,
Then my little soul's going to shine along.

I'm going to climb up Jacob's ladder,
I'm going to climb up higher and higher,
I'm going to sit down at the welcome table,
I'm going to feast off milk and honey,
I'm going to tell God how-a you starved me,
I'm going to join the big baptizing.

Then my little soul's going to shine, shine,
Then my little soul's going to shine along.

Open the Window, Noah!

THE STORY OF NOAH AND THE FLOOD WAS ESPECIALLY APPEALING TO *the slave poets, perhaps because it described the destruction of a corrupt and sinful world, a cataclysm the enslaved could only hope would reoccur. In this spiritual, the lyrics urge Noah to let the dove into the ark with its olive leaf, the promise of a cleansed, redeemed, and free world.*

Open the window, Noah!
Open the window, Noah!
Open the window, Noah!
Open the window,
Let the dove come in.

The little dove flew in the window and
    mourned,
Open the window,
Let the dove come in.

The little dove brought back the olive leaf,
Open the window,
Let the dove come in.

Open the window, Noah!
Open the window, Noah!
Open the window, Noah!
Open the window,
Let the dove come in.

Rain Fall and Wet Becca Lawton

W E S H A L L N E V E R K N O W W H O B E C C A L A W T O N W A S , N O R S H A L L W E E V E R *know the story of her being wet by the rain and why that seemingly meaningless event was written into a song. But she is immortalized in this charming spiritual. These spontaneous, improvised songs were about real people, real happenings, real life; they were, in fact, storytelling through music. Like folk tales and blues songs, spirituals, as the novelist Richard Wright has said, were "recounted from mouth to mouth . . . [and] formed the channels through which the racial wisdom flowed."*

Rain fall and wet Becca Lawton,
O, rain fall and wet Becca Lawton,
O! Brother, cry holy!

Do, Becca Lawton, come to me yonder,
Say, brother Tony, what shall I do now?
Beat back holy and rock salvation.

Rain fall and wet Becca Lawton,
O, rain fall and wet Becca Lawton,
O! Brother, cry holy!

Rise Up, Shepherd, and Follow

STARS, SHEPHERDS, HERDS, AND FLOCKS WERE INTIMATELY FAMILIAR TO *slave laborers on Southern farms and plantations. And runaway slaves traveled by night, guided by the North Star and other heavenly formations, as they made their slow and perilous way north to freedom. This song tells their story, and it was honored in 1933 by Tuskegee Institute in Alabama when the song's title and imagery was chosen for one of the stained-glass chapel windows devoted to a number of major spirituals.*

There's a star in the east on Christmas
    morn,
Rise up, shepherd, and follow;
It'll lead to the place where the Savior's
    born,
Rise up, shepherd, and follow.

If you take good heed to the angels' words,
Rise up, shepherd, and follow;
You'll forget your flocks, you'll forget your
    herds,

Rise up, shepherd, and follow.
Leave your sheep and leave your lambs,
Rise up, shepherd, and follow;
Leave your ewes and leave your rams,
Rise up, shepherd, and follow;
Follow, follow,
Follow the star of Bethlehem,
Rise up, shepherd, and follow.

Swing Low, Sweet Chariot

ONE OF THE CLASSIC SPIRITUALS, "SWING LOW, SWEET CHARIOT" CAN *be read in several ways. The overt meaning is clearly religious. As music historian John Lovell, Jr., writes, "This is one of a family of songs in which a great golden vehicle, powered and directed by God, manned by angels, comes down from heaven and through the skies to pick up and elevate a particular individual." But God's liberation also works in this world, and "carry me home" could mean escape from enslavement by returning to Africa or by finding freedom in Canada.*

Swing low, sweet char-i-ot, Com-ing for to car-ry me home,

Swing low, sweet char-i-ot, Com-ing for to car-ry me home.

FINE.

1. I looked o - ver Jor-dan, and what did I see,
2. If you get there be - fore I do,
3. The bright - est day that ev - er I saw,
4. I'm some - times up and some - times down,

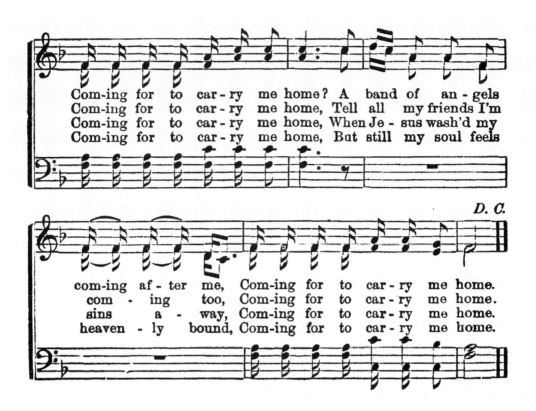

D. C.

Com-ing for to car-ry me home? A band of an-gels
Com-ing for to car-ry me home, Tell all my friends I'm
Com-ing for to car-ry me home, When Je-sus wash'd my
Com-ing for to car-ry me home, But still my soul feels

com-ing af-ter me, Com-ing for to car-ry me home.
com - ing too, Com-ing for to car-ry me home.
sins a - way, Com-ing for to car-ry me home.
heaven - ly bound, Com-ing for to car-ry me home.

Somebody's Calling My Name

IN THE MIDST OF THE CIVIL WAR SLAVES WHO HAD ESCAPED AND RUN *away to the safety of the Union army lines were protected as the contraband of war by General Benjamin Butler at Fortress Monroe. It was here that sympathetic whites heard spirituals sung, often for the first time. A notice signed only "C. W. D." in Dwight's Journal of Music reported, "It is one of the most striking incidents of the war to listen to the singing of a group of colored people at Fortress Monroe." This is one of the songs that so moved and impressed the antislavery soldiers.*

Hush, O, hush,
Somebody's calling my name,
Hush, O, hush,
Somebody's calling my name,
Hush, O, hush,
Somebody's calling my name,
O, my Lord,
O, my Lord,
What shall I do?

I'm so glad
I got my religion in time,
I'm so glad
I got my religion in time,
O, my Lord,
O, my Lord,
What shall I do?

Soon I Will Be Done

IN THIS EDENIC VISION OF "HOME" TROUBLES AND WEEPING ARE OVER *at long last, families separated by the auction block are reunited, and everyone is protected by a loving God. This song exemplifies the meaning of the spirituals as defined by their great modern interpreter, Marian Anderson. Spirituals are, she said, "a conversation, a wish, a prayer from one soul to another."*

Soon I will be done with the troubles of the
    world,
Troubles of the world, the troubles of the
    world,
Soon I will be done with the troubles of the
    world,
Going home to live with God.

No more weeping and wailing,
No more weeping and wailing,
No more weeping and wailing,
I'm going to live with God.

I want to meet my mother,
I want to meet my mother,
I want to meet my mother,
I'm going to live with God.

I want to meet my Jesus,
I want to meet my Jesus,
I want to meet my Jesus,
I'm going to live with God.

This Is the Way I Pray

These lyrics show that slave families prayed, sang, and wor-shipped in their cabins as well as in the meeting houses or secret brush arbors where the black community worshipped together.

This is the way I pray in my home,
This is the way I pray in my home,
This is the way I pray in my home,
I pray like this:
"Lord, have mercy."

This is the way I sing in my home,
This is the way I sing in my home,
This is the way I sing in my home,
I sing like this:
"Praise His name."

This is the way I moan in my home,
This is the way I moan in my home,
This is the way I moan in my home,
I moan just like this:
"Mmmmmmmmmmmmmmmmmm."

This is the way I pray in my home,
This is the way I pray in my home,
This is the way I pray in my home,
I pray just like this:
"Lord, have mercy."

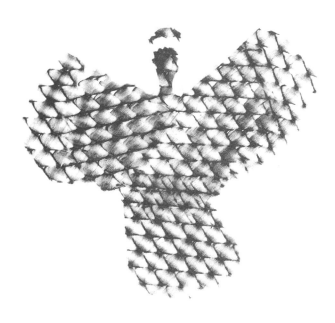

Walk Together, Children

THE VISION OF A PROMISED LAND—CANADA, AFRICA, LIBERIA, THE FREE *North, Heaven—inspired African-American slaves to keep going. The mutual encouragement of African Americans and the constant realization of the necessity of unity kept people moving forward in their continuing struggle. "Walk together, children" has become a phrase of group solidarity and support within the black community.*

Walk together, children,
Don't you get weary,
Walk together, children,
Don't you get weary,
O, walk together children,
Don't you get weary,
There's a great camp meeting
In the promised land.

Going to mourn and never tire,
Mourn and never tire,
Mourn and never tire.
There's a great camp meeting
In the Promised Land.

O, sing together, children, children,
Don't you get weary,
Sing together, children,
Don't you get weary, children.

Stand together, children, children,
Don't you get weary,
There's a great camp meeting
In that Promised Land;
O, walk together,
Keep on a-walking,
There's a great camp meeting
In that Promised Land.

I'm a Poor Wayfaring Stranger

THE METAPHOR OF LIFE AS A JOURNEY IS NOT UNFAMILIAR IN THE *world's literature; the image of life as a pilgrimage, however, cuts deeper. Deeper yet is the trope sung by an enslaved people who have been cut off from their history and culture, and whose future in exile is full of danger. "I'm a poor, wayfaring stranger," indeed. Nonetheless, this song surges with hope: "I'm just going over Jordan."*

I'm a poor, wayfaring stranger,
While journeying through this world of
　　woe,
Yet there's no sickness, toil, and danger,
In that bright world to which I go;
I'm going there to see my father,
I'm going there no more to roam,
I'm just going over Jordan,
I'm just going over home.

I know dark clouds will gather 'round me,
I know my way is rough and steep,
Yet bright fields lie just before me,
Where God's redeemed their vigils keep;
I'm going there to see my mother,
She said she'd meet me when I come,
I'm just going over Jordan,
I'm just going over home.

I'll soon be free from every trial,
My body will sleep in the old churchyard,
I'll drop the cross of self-denial,
And enter on my great reward;
I'm going there to see my Savior,
To sing His praise in Heaven's dome,
I'm just going over Jordan,
I'm just going over home.

When the Saints Come Marchin' In

THIS SPIRITUAL BECAME FAMOUS WHEN THE MUSIC WAS "RAGGED" IN *New Orleans in the 1890s, and it became a standard number in the new musical creation called jazz. The best jazz rendition is by Louis Armstrong, the musical genius who transformed jazz from a local to an international phenomenon and from the vernacular into high art.*

When the saints come marchin' in,
When the saints come marchin' in,
Lord, I want to be in that number
When the saints come marchin' in.

I have a lovin' brother,
He is gone on before.
And I promised I would meet Him
When they crown Him Lord of all.

When they crown Him Lord of all,
When they crown Him Lord of all,
Lord, I want to be in that number
When they crown Him Lord of all,

I have a loving sister,
She is gone on before.
And I promised I would meet her
When they gather 'round the throne.

When they gather 'round the throne,
When they gather 'round the throne,
Lord, I want to be in that number
When they gather 'round the throne.

Songs of the

spirit

Keep Me from Sinking Down

THE LYRICS OF THIS SPIRITUAL CONSTITUTE A PRAYER TO GOD FOR *help and a rallying cry in the face of the inhumane treatment of the slave system. The songs of the community helped African Americans to strengthen their resistance to oppression and to keep them from "sinking down." Religion was empowering; ironically, as the scholar and poet Sterling Brown remarked of the slave owners, "They taught you the religion they disgraced."*

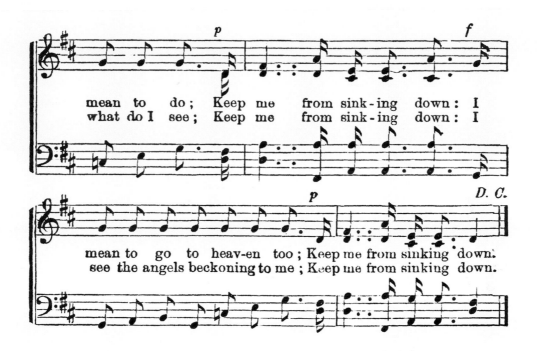

mean to do; Keep me from sink-ing down: I
what do I see; Keep me from sink-ing down: I

mean to go to heav-en too; Keep me from sinking down.
see the angels beckoning to me; Keep me from sinking down.

When I was a mourner just like you;
Keep me from sinking down:
I mourned and mourned till I got through;
Keep me from sinking down.
Chorus: O, Lord . . .

I bless the Lord I'm going to die;
Keep me from sinking down:
I'm going to judgment by and by;
Keep me from sinking down.
Chorus: O, Lord . . .

Holy Bible

SPIRITUALS WERE KNOWN IN THE WHITE SOUTH BEFORE THE CIVIL *War, but they were little noted or appreciated. One exception comes from the diary of British-born actress Fanny Kemble, the wife of a slaveholder, who described attending an African-American funeral in 1839: "The whole congregation uplifted their voices in a hymn, the first high wailing notes of which—sung all in unison— sent a thrill through all my nerves."*

Holy Bible, Holy Bible,
Holy Bible, book divine, book divine;
O, what weeping, O, what weeping,
O, what weeping over me, over me;

Weeping Mary, weeping Mary,
Weep no more, weep no more.

Before I'd be a slave, I'd be buried in my
   grave,
And go home to my Father and be saved.

Doubting Thomas, doubting Thomas,
Doubting Thomas, doubt no more, doubt
   no more;
Great Jehovah, Great Jehovah,
Great Jehovah, over all, over all.

Before I'd be a slave, I'd be buried in my
   grave,
And go home to my Father and be saved.

Didn't It Rain!

ON JULY 7, 1958, THE GREAT GOSPEL SINGER MAHALIA JACKSON WAS
*scheduled to present an outdoor concert in Newport, Rhode Island. Thousands
waited in the pouring rain to hear her sing, and her first number was "Didn't It
Rain!" Rudi Blesch, the music historian, commented, "Our time had never heard it
sung like that. . . . No one within our memory has rocked the old songs—so mirac-
ulously and sweetly distilled from the bitterness of servitude—as she rocks them."*

O, didn't it rain, children,
Didn't it rain!
Didn't it rain, children,
Didn't it rain!

Didn't it rain, children,
Didn't it rain, children,
Didn't it rain, children,
Didn't it rain!

Do Don't You Weep for the Baby

THE SLAVES' MORTALITY RATE WAS HIGH, AND MANY AFRICAN-AMERICAN
*babies died because their mothers were overworked, malnourished, and lacked med-
ical attention. Only a few parents can ever fully know what it means to lose a child,
but this poignant spiritual communicates the depth of that sorrow.*

Do don't you weep for the baby,
My heart,
O, my heart.
Do don't you weep for the baby,
For my heart's so sorry.

Do don't you weep for the baby,
My heart,
O, my heart.
Do don't you weep for the baby,
For my heart's so sorry.

The Downward Road Is Crowded

THE FAVORITE TEXT OF THE WHITE MINISTERS WHOM THE SLAVE OWNERS *sent to preach to the slaves was "Servants, obey your masters." Every plantation slave had heard many exhortations based on those four words of scripture. The slave community, however, fully comprehended the whites' distortion of the Bible and countered it with the radically Christian concept that one should be obedient to God alone. The slaves sought to avoid the crowded downward road.*

O, the downward road is crowded,
Crowded, crowded,
O, the downward road is crowded,
With unbelieving souls.

Come, all ye wayward travelers,
And let us all join and sing,
The everlasting praises,
Of Jesus Christ our King.

Old Satan's mighty busy,
He follows me night and day,
And everywhere I'm appointed,
There's something in my way.

When I was a sinner
I loved my distance well,
But when I came to find myself,
I was hanging over Hell.

O, the downward road is crowded,
Crowded, crowded,
O, the downward road is crowded,
With unbelieving souls.

Every Time I Feel the Spirit

Robert Russa Moton, the principal of Tuskegee Institute, wrote in 1909 that the spirituals are not merely poetry: "They are life itself in the life of the human soul." "Every time I feel the spirit moving in my heart I will pray" are profound words of the soul.

Every time I feel the spirit moving in my
heart I will pray,
Every time I feel the spirit moving in my
heart I will pray.

Upon the mountain my Lord spoke,
Out of His mouth came fire and smoke;
All around me looks so fine,

Asked my Lord if all was mine;
Jordan river is chilly and cold,
Chills the body but not the soul.

Every time I feel the spirit moving in my
heart I will pray,
Every time I feel the spirit moving in my
heart I will pray.

Give Up the World

The world of slaveholding America was one of moral corruption, religious hypocrisy, human exploitation, financial greed, class arrogance, and racial superiority. Little wonder this spiritual calls upon pretenders and backsliders to pray a little longer, listen to Jesus, and give up their tainted allegiance to a wicked world.

My brother, won't you give up the world,
My brother, won't you give up the world,
My brother, won't you give up the world,
Hear what my Jesus say?
Pray a little longer, give up the world,
Pray a little longer, give up the world.

Pretender, won't you give up the world,
Backslider, won't you give up the world,
Hypocrite, won't you give up the world,
Hear what my Jesus say?
Pray a little longer, give up the world,
Pray a little longer, give up the world.

Go, Mary, and Toll the Bell

THIS SONG ENVISIONS AND ANTICIPATES A GREAT GATHERING, EITHER IN *Heaven or in freedom, with a roll call of God's people. Myth and history, past and present, are intertwined here as African Americans interpret their own experiences through what music scholar Jon Michael Spencer calls "the biblical lens." The slaves saw themselves as God's chosen people of their own time, united with God's ancient people of Israel. Verses based on various colors of clothing turn up again in the blues.*

Go, Mary, and toll the bell,
Come, John, and call the roll,
I thank God.
Who's all them come dressed in white?
They must be the children of the Israelite.
Who's all them come dressed in red?
They must be the children that Moses led.
Who's all them come dressed in blue?
They must be the children just come through.
Who's all them come dressed in black?
They must be the mourners just turned back.
Go, Mary, and toll the bell,
Come, John, and call the roll,
I thank God.

He Never Said a Mumbling Word

JESUS' SCOURGING WAS A BIBLICAL EVENT WITH WHICH AFRICAN *Americans could fully identify. The whip was the slave masters' chief method of controlling men and women at work and punishing slaves who broke the owners' arbitrary rules. Advertisements for runaways in Southern newspapers often included grisly descriptions of scarred backs and maimed limbs. Not crying out despite the pain during a whipping of thirty or fifty or a hundred lashes was one of the slaves' methods of holding on to their dignity and demonstrating resistance.*

O, they whipped Him up the hill, up the hill,
up the hill,
O, they whipped Him up the hill, and He
never said a mumbling word,
O, they whipped Him up the hill, and He
never said a mumbling word,
He just hung down His head, and He cried.

O, they crowned Him with a thorny crown,
thorny crown, thorny crown,
O, they crowned Him with a thorny crown,
and He never said a mumbling word,
O, they crowned Him with a thorny crown,
and He never said a mumbling word,
He just hung down His head, and He
cried.

Well, they nailed Him to the cross, to the
cross, to the cross,
Well, they nailed Him to the cross, and He
never said a mumbling word,
Well, they nailed Him to the cross, and He
never said a mumbling word,
He just hung down His head, and He cried.

Well, they pierced Him in the side, in the
side, in the side,
Well, they pierced Him in the side, and the
blood came a-twinkling down,
Well, they pierced Him in the side, and the
blood came a-twinkling down,
Then He just hung down His head, and He
died.

Mary and Martha

"MARY AND MARTHA" IS ONE OF THE LOVELIEST AFRICAN-AMERICAN *spirituals. The poetically colorful adjective* charming *is probably a variation of* chiming. *Large southern plantations had bells that summoned slaves to never-ending work, so the contrasting image of bells "crying free grace and dying love" is a hopeful vision of a future free from oppression.*

1. Ma-ry and a Martha's just gone 'long, Ma-ry and a Martha's just gone 'long, Ma-ry and a Mar-tha's just gone 'long, To ring those charming bells; Cry-ing free grace and dy-ing love,

Free grace and dy-ing love, Free grace and dy-ing love, To ring those charming bells. Oh! way o-ver Jordan, Lord, Way o-ver Jordan, Lord, Way over Jordan, Lord, To ring those charming bells.

The preacher and the elder's just gone
    'long . . .
To ring those charming bells.
Chorus: Crying free grace . . .

My father and mother's just gone 'long . . .
To ring those charming bells.
Chorus: Crying free grace . . .

The Methodist and Baptist's just gone
    'long . . .
To ring those charming bells.
Chorus: Crying free grace . . .

I Couldn't Hear Nobody Pray

AFRICAN-AMERICAN MUSICIAN AND PRODUCER QUINCY JONES HAS SAID, *"A lot of history is in the words, and some words don't mean what you think." Whether in the valley or in the Kingdom or "way down yonder," the African-American slave had to fight to create his or her own personal space. Slavery prescribed every detail of African-American life, so maintaining identity and integrity was a constant but imperative struggle. "I couldn't hear nobody pray" speaks of the solitude of the struggle.*

In the valley on my knees!
With my burden and my Savior!
And I couldn't hear nobody pray,
O, way down yonder by myself,
And I couldn't hear nobody pray.

Chilly waters in the Jordan!
Crossing over into Canaan!
And I couldn't hear nobody pray,
O, way down yonder by myself,
And I couldn't hear nobody pray.

Hallelujah! Troubles over!
In the Kingdom with my Jesus!
And I couldn't hear nobody pray,
O, way down yonder by myself,
And I couldn't hear nobody pray.

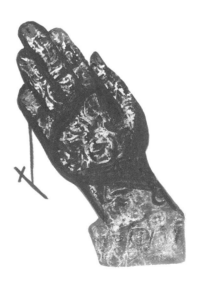

Children, Did You Hear When Jesus Rose?

PART OF THE GENIUS OF THE SPIRITUALS IS THEIR VIBRANT USE OF VER-
*nacular English. "Mary set her table / In spite of all her foes" are lines of real orig-
inality and folk vitality. They merit James Weldon Johnson's tribute to the slave
poets, whom he called the "black and unknown bards of long ago."*

Children, did you hear when Jesus rose?
Did you hear when Jesus rose?
Children, did you hear when Jesus rose?
He rose and ascended on high!

Mary set her table
In spite of all her foes;
King Jesus sat at the center place
And cups did overflow.

The Father looked at His Son and smiled,
The Son did look at-a Him;
The Father saved my soul from Hell
And the Son freed me from sin.

The Hypocrite and the Concubine

THIS SPIRITUAL SHOWS THE SLAVE POET'S IMAGINATIVE USE OF LAN-
*guage to create arresting images. Thomas Wentworth Higginson, one of the first
white abolitionists to hear and appreciate spirituals, once asked an African-
American oarsman how the words of these extraordinary songs were composed. The
answer was: "Just putting a word and then another word."*

Hypocrite and the concubine,
Living among the swine,
They run to God with lips and tongue,
And leave all the heart behind.

Aunty, did you hear when Jesus rose?
Did you hear when Jesus rose?
Aunty, did you hear when Jesus rose?
He rose and He ascended on high.

Death Is Going to Lay His Cold Icy Hands on Me

ALTHOUGH THIS SEEMS TO BE A SONG ABOUT DEATH, IT IS ALSO A CODED *message about running away: "You'll look for me and I'll be gone." In addition, it predicts a coming cataclysm: "Yes, one of these mornings about twelve o'clock / This old world's going to reel and rock." These words may signal a slave uprising.*

Death is going to lay his cold icy hands on
   me,
Death is going to lay his cold icy hands on
   me.
One morning I was walking along,
I heard a voice and saw no man;
Said go in peace and sin no more,
Your sins forgiven and your soul set free.

One of these mornings it won't be long,
You'll look for me and I'll be gone,
Yes, one of these mornings about twelve
   o'clock
This old world's going to reel and rock.

Death is going to lay his cold icy hands on
   me,
Death is going to lay his cold icy hands on
   me, Lord!

I Can't Stand the Fire

ONE OF THE EARLIEST PEOPLE TO WRITE ABOUT THE DISTINCTIVE *quality of African-American spirituals was Levi Coffin of North Carolina, who mentioned hearing the slaves sing "one of their plantation songs, or hymns" in 1821. Coffin described the song as "a sort of prayer in rhyme, in which the same words appear again and again." This spiritual fits his description.*

I can't stand the fire,
Dear sister, I can't stand the fire,
While Jordan there rolls so swift.
I can't stand the fire,
Dear sister, I can't stand the fire,

O Lord, I can't stand the fire,
While Jordan there rolls so swift.

I Got a Mother in the Bright Shinin' World

THE AFRICAN-AMERICAN ACTOR AND ACTIVIST PAUL ROBESON WAS *one of the great twentieth-century singers of spirituals. His granddaughter, Susan Robeson, pinpointed the meaning of these songs for the slaves: "They sang to forget the chains and misery. The sorrow will one day turn to joy. All that breaks the heart and oppresses the soul will one day give place to peace and understanding, and every man will be free. That is the interpretation of a true Negro spiritual." That is the "bright shinin' world" of this song.*

I got a mother in the bright shinin' world,
I got a mother in the bright shinin' world,
Dear Mother, I hope to meet you over there
In the bright shinin' world.
In the bright shinin' world,
In the bright shinin' world,
I hope to meet you over there
In the bright shinin' world.

I got a father in the bright shinin' world,
I got a father in the bright shinin' world,
Dear Father, I hope to meet you over there
In the bright shinin' world.

Jesus call me in the bright shinin' world,
Jesus call me in the bright shinin' world,
I hope to meet Him over there
In the bright shinin' world.

I Saw the Beam in My Sister's Eye

In 1914, THE MUSIC HISTORIAN HENRY E. KREHBIEL PUBLISHED *AFRO-American Folksongs, an early and sympathetic presentation of black music. He wrote, "The songs of the black slaves of the South are original and native products. They contain idioms which were transplanted hither from Africa, but as songs they are the product of American institutions; of the social, political, and geographical environment . . . of the joys, sorrows, and experiences which fell to their lot in America." The use of the Bible in this spiritual shows the unique nature of black song.*

I saw the beam in my sister's eye,
Couldn't see the beam in mine;
You'd better leave your sister's door,
Go keep your own door clean.

And I had a mighty battle like Jacob and the
　　angel,
Jacob, time of old;
I didn't intend to let him go
Till Jesus blessed my soul.

And blessed me, and blessed me,
And blessed all my soul;
I didn't intend to let him go
Till Jesus blessed my soul.

I Want to Die Like-a Lazarus

ACCORDING TO THE NEW TESTAMENT STORY, LAZARUS IS THE PERSON *Jesus raised from the dead. To die like Lazarus died, therefore, is to die not for some future life in Heaven, but to be resurrected, inspired, transformed, in order to live this life on earth. White scholars have traditionally interpreted the spirituals as otherworldly, believing the slaves were satisfied in their servitude, but these lyrics show the slaves' passionate commitment to life here and now.*

I want to die like-a Lazarus died,
Die like-a Lazarus died;
I want to die like-a Lazarus died,
Like-a Lazarus died,
Like-a Lazarus died.

Roll, Jordan, Roll

ONE OF THE MOST FAMILIAR SPIRITUALS, "ROLL, JORDAN, ROLL" PROB-
*ably began as a boatmen's song, with the rhythmic refrains setting the pace for the
oars. When she heard this spiritual while teaching freedpeople after the Civil War,
the African-American abolitionist Charlotte Forten Grimké wrote, "I never listen to
'Roll, Jordan, Roll' without seeming to hear, almost to feel, the rolling of waters."
In 1867, when* Slave Songs of the United States *was published, "Roll, Jordan,
Roll" was the first song in this first compilation of spirituals.*

Roll, Jordan, roll,   roll, Jordan, roll, I want to go to

Roll, . . .

hea -ven when I die, To hear Jor - dan roll.

1. Oh, brothers, you ought t'have been there, Yes, my Lord! A sit-ting in the Kingdom, To hear Jor-dan roll.

O, preachers, you ought t'have been
   there . . .

O, sinners, you ought . . .

O, mourners, you ought . . .

O, seekers, you ought . . .

O, mothers, you ought . . .

O, sisters, you ought . . .

I'm All Wore Out a-Toiling for the Lord

THIS SPIRITUAL IS A HYMN OF INVITATION, CALLING WAYWARD SINNERS *to repentance: "Come on . . . there is time to save." The slave poet may be "all wore out a-toiling for the Lord," but he or she, rather than being afraid, is "ready to go" to Jerusalem, either the heavenly city or an earthly paradise of freedom.*

I'm all wore out a-toiling for the Lord,
My bones done tremble on the brink of the
　　grave,
O Jerusalem is nigh,
And I ain't a bit afraid.

Come on, sinner,
There is time to save.
Come on, sinner, come!
Come on, sinner, come!
O, O,
Come on, sinner, come!

I'm all wore out a-toiling for the Lord,
My days are numbered and I'm ready to go,
In the evening time
I pray to see the open door.

Come on, sinner,
There is time to save.
Come on, sinner, come!
Come on, sinner, come!
O, O,
Come on, sinner, come!

I've Been 'Buked

THIS CLASSIC SPIRITUAL REPORTS SLAVERY'S HUMILIATION OF MEN AND *women. The conservative African-American leader Booker T. Washington wrote, "Nothing tells more truly what the Negro's life in slavery was, than the songs in which he succeeded . . . in expressing his deepest thoughts and feelings."*

I've been 'buked and I've been scorned,
O, Lord—
I've been 'buked and I've been scorned,
Children—
I've been 'buked and I've been scorned,
I've been talked about sure's you're born.

But, ain't goin' to lay my religion down,
No, Lord—
Ain't goin' to lay my religion down,
Children—
No, ain't goin' to lay my religion down,
Ain't goin' to lay my religion down.

I'm a Everyday Witness

IN THE FIRST HALF OF THE TWENTIETH CENTURY, A SERIOUS CONTRO-
*versy divided those who saw the African origins and African-American creativity of
the spirituals from those who believed that they were merely imitations of European
folk songs and hymns. As Mary Jo Sanna, the musicologist, points out, white
people tried to co-opt the origins of the spirituals by claiming they were only derivative. Since that time scholarship has definitively demonstrated the retention and
persistence of elements of African culture in America, and the inventiveness of
African-American culture. The lyrics and rhythm of "I'm a Everyday Witness"
reflect that combination.*

I'm a witness for my Lord,
I'm a witness for my Lord,
I'm a witness for my Lord,
I'm a everyday witness for my Lord.

I'm a Monday witness for my Lord,
I'm a Monday witness for my Lord,
I'm a Monday witness for my Lord,
I'm a everyday witness for my Lord.

I'm a Tuesday witness for my Lord,
I'm a Tuesday witness for my Lord,
I'm a Tuesday witness for my Lord,
I'm a everyday witness for my Lord.

I'm a Wednesday witness for my Lord,
I'm a Wednesday witness for my Lord,
I'm a Wednesday witness for my Lord,
I'm a everyday witness for my Lord.

I'm a Thursday witness for my Lord,
I'm a Thursday witness for my Lord,
I'm a Thursday witness for my Lord,
I'm a everyday witness for my Lord.

I'm a Friday witness for my Lord,
I'm a Friday witness for my Lord,
I'm a Friday witness for my Lord,
I'm a everyday witness for my Lord.

I'm a Saturday witness for my Lord,
I'm a Saturday witness for my Lord,
I'm a Saturday witness for my Lord,
I'm a everyday witness for my Lord.

In the Army of the Lord

WITH THIS IMAGE OF AN ARMY, THE AFRICAN-AMERICAN SLAVES POR-
*tray themselves as a mighty band under divine leadership engaged in the great bat-
tle for righteousness. Their participation in this army will never die, for their spirit
is constantly reborn. But theirs is no otherworldly struggle: "I'm fightin' for my
rights in this army." The time for justice is always now.*

I'm a soldier in the army of the Lord,
I'm a soldier in the army;
I'm a soldier in the army of the Lord,
I'm a soldier in the army.
I'll live again in the army of the Lord,
I'll live again in this army;
I'll live again in the army of the Lord,
I'll live again in this army.

If a man dies in the army of the Lord,
If a man dies in this army;
If a man dies in the army of the Lord,
If a man dies in this army.
He'll live again in the army of the Lord,
He'll live again in this army;
He'll live again in the army of the Lord,
He'll live again in this army.

I've had a hard time in the army of the Lord,
Had a hard time in this army;
I've had a hard time in the army of the Lord,
Had a hard time in this army.
I'm fightin' for my rights in the army of the
    Lord,
I'm fightin' for my rights in this army;
I'm fightin' for my rights in the army of the
    Lord,
I'm fightin' for my rights in this army.

I've come a long way in the army of the
    Lord,
Come a long way in this army;
I've come a long way in the army of the
    Lord,
Come a long way in this army.
Someday I'll rest in the army of the Lord,
Someday I'll rest in this army;
Someday I'll rest in the army of the Lord,
Someday I'll rest in this army.

My soul died in the army of the Lord,
My soul died in this army;
My soul died in the army of the Lord,
My soul died in this army.
It'll live again in the army of the Lord,
It'll live again in this army;
It'll live again in the army of the Lord,
It'll live again in this army.

Hosanna, in the army of the Lord,
Hosanna, in this army;
Hosanna, in the army of the Lord,
Hosanna, in this army.
We'll live again in the army of the Lord,
We'll live again in this army;
We'll live again in the army of the Lord,
We'll live again in this army.

My mother died in the army of the Lord,
My mother died in this army;
My mother died in the army of the Lord,
My mother died in this army.

She'll live again in the army of the Lord,
She'll live again in this army;
She'll live again in the army of the Lord,
She'll live again in this army.

I'm Working on the Building

MANY SLAVES WERE SKILLED CRAFTSPEOPLE, SUCH AS IRONWORKERS *and carpenters. In this spiritual the building is a metaphor for the kingdom of God, and the work being done is the construction by humans of a reign of freedom, justice, and peace on earth. James M. McKim, an early commentator on the spirituals, wrote in 1862 that "they tell the whole story of these peoples' life and character."*

I'm working on the building for my Lord,
For my Lord, for my Lord,
I'm working on the building for my Lord,
For my Lord, for my Lord,
I'm working on the building for my Lord,
Working on the building too.

If I was a sinner, I tell you what I would do,
I'd throw away my sinful ways and work on
    the building too;
If I was a dancer, I tell you what I would do,

I'd throw away my dancing shoes and work
    on the building too;
If I was a gambler, I tell you what I would
    do,
I'd throw away my gambling dice and work
    on the building too.

I'm working on the building for my Lord,
For my Lord, for my Lord,
I'm working on the building for my Lord,
For my Lord, for my Lord.

I'm in Trouble

Perhaps the most important essay written on the spirituals is *W. E. B. Du Bois's "Of the Sorrow Songs," a chapter in his classic* The Souls of Black Folk, *first published in 1903. He begins his essay, "They that walked in darkness sang songs in the olden days—Sorrow Songs—for they were weary at heart. . . . Ever since I was a child these songs have stirred me strangely. They came out of the South unknown to me, one by one, and yet at once I knew them as of me and of mine." This song is a testimony to Du Bois's words.*

I'm in trouble, Lord,
I'm in trouble,
I'm in trouble, Lord,
Trouble about my grave.

Sometimes I weep,
Sometimes I mourn,
I'm in trouble about my grave;
Sometimes I can't do neither one,
I'm in trouble about my grave.

John Done Saw That Number

THE AFRICAN-AMERICAN TENOR ROLAND HAYES WAS ONE OF THE GREAT *modern singers of spirituals in the early twentieth century. At his first concert before a white audience, however, in Lexington, Kentucky, he was forced to sing standing behind a curtain because of the city's racial segregation laws. African Americans and their special heritage are less invisible today than they once were. Spirituals are now well established as the foundation of black music, the progenitor of gospel, early blues, New Orleans brass bands, and jazz itself.*

John done saw that number,
'Way in the middle of the air;
Don't you wanta join that number,
'Way in the middle of the air?

On the right I saw a sight,
'Way in the middle of the air;
A band of angels dressed in white,
'Way in the middle of the air.

Havin' great tribulations,
'Way in the middle of the air;
Havin' their harps in their hand's,
'Way in the middle of the air.

Singin' a new song before the throne,
'Way in the middle of the air;
That angels in Heaven could not sing,
'Way in the middle of the air.

John done saw that number,
'Way in the middle of the air;
Comin' up from hard trials,
'Way in the middle of the air.

On the left I saw no rest,
'Way in the middle of the air;
I'm gonna talk about God myself,
'Way in the middle of the air.

There's a Meeting Here Tonight

T HIS SINGABLE, ENTHUSIASTIC CAMP MEETING SONG COMES FROM THE
*days when the Methodists were among the leading evangelicals. This spiritual
was later adapted by the labor movement to encourage organizational meetings of
union members.*

Get you rea - dy, there's a meet-ing here to-night, Come a -
long, there's a meet-ing here to-night; I know you by your
dai - ly walk, There's a meeting here to-night. 1. Camp-meeting

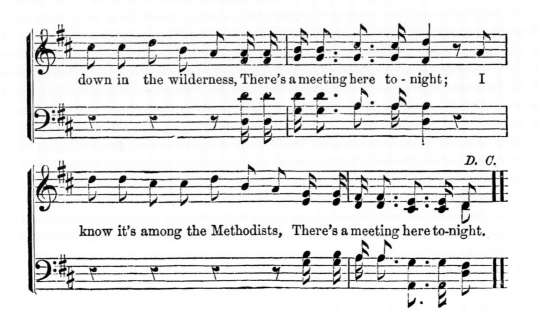

down in the wilderness, There's a meeting here to-night; I know it's among the Methodists, There's a meeting here to-night.

Those angels' wings are tipped with
    gold . . .
That brought glad tidings to my soul . . .

My father says it is the best . . .
To live and die a Methodist . . .

I'm a Methodist bred and a Methodist
    born . . .
And when I'm dead there's a Methodist
    gone . . .

King Jesus Is My Only Friend

THE BLACK MUSIC AND THEATER CRITIC THEOPHILUS LEWIS CLAIMS THAT *often it is the spiritual as poem rather than as melody that gives the song its strength and significance. As poems, the spirituals draw their power from their simple sincerity and directness, as well as their innovative use of language and astonishingly creative imagery. "King Jesus Is My Only Friend" is a striking example.*

King Jesus is my only friend,
King Jesus is my only friend,
King Jesus is my only friend,
King Jesus is my only friend.

When the doctor, the doctor done give me
over,
When the doctor, the doctor done give me
over,
When the doctor, the doctor done give me
over,
King Jesus is my only friend.

When the preacher, the preacher done give
me over,
King Jesus is my only friend.
When my house, my house become a public
hall,
King Jesus is my only friend.
When my face, my face become a looking
glass,
King Jesus is my only friend.

Let the Church Roll On

THE BLACK CHURCH WAS THE SINGLE EARLY AFRICAN-AMERICAN INSTI-
*tution that was not under white control. It was the church that preserved elements of
African culture, that served as the center for community life and leadership, and
that provided a solid base for the nurturing and expression of black culture.*

Let the church roll on, my Lord,
Let the church roll on, my Lord,
You can put the Devil out, my Lord,
Let the church roll on, my Lord,

If there's preachers in the church, my Lord,
And they're not living right, my Lord;
Just turn the preachers out, my Lord,
And let the church roll on.

If there's members in the church, my Lord,
And they're not living right, my Lord;
You can put the members out, my Lord,
And let the church roll on.

If there's liars in the church, my Lord,
And they're not living right, my Lord;
You can put the liars out, my Lord,
And let the church roll on.

If there's sinners in the church, my Lord,
And they're not living right, my Lord;
Just put the sinners out, my Lord,
And let the church roll on.

Let Us Cheer the Weary Traveler

"THESE SONGS," W. E. B. DU BOIS WROTE, "ARE THE ARTICULATE MESsage of the slave to the world." The spirituals were the voice of an enslaved people, allowing them to speak beyond the confines of their prison walls. The spirituals were also communications within the African-American community itself. This spiritual, for example, is a song of morale building, mutual support, and solidarity.

Let us cheer the weary traveler,
Cheer the weary traveler;
Let us cheer the weary traveler,
Along the heavenly way.

I'll take my gospel trumpet,
And I'll begin to blow,
And if my Savior helps me,
I'll blow wherever I go.

And if you meet with crosses,
And trials on the way,
Just keep your trust in Jesus,
And don't forget to pray.

Let us cheer the weary traveler,
Cheer the weary traveler;
Let us cheer the weary traveler,
Along the heavenly way.

Mary Had a Baby, Yes, Lord

TWO OF THE MANY NEW TESTAMENT IMAGES OF JESUS FREQUENTLY *appear in the spirituals. One highlights the vulnerable human innocence of Mary's baby. The other depicts a king who rules with freedom and justice, in contrast to the oppressive slaveholders. This song combines both representations and concludes with an unexpected twist.*

Mary had a baby,
Yes, Lord!
Mary had a baby,
Yes, Lord!
Mary had a baby,
Yes, Lord!
The people keep a-coming
And the train done gone.

Mary had a baby,
Yes, Lord!

What did she name him?
She named him King Jesus,
She named him Mighty Counselor.
Where was he born?
Born in a manger,
Yes, Lord!

Mary had a baby,
Yes, Lord!
The people keep a-coming
and the train done gone.

Michael, Row the Boat Ashore

SUNG IN CONTEMPORARY TIMES BY HARRY BELAFONTE AND OTHERS, *this spiritual has crossed over to become a popular American folk ballad. Originally, it was undoubtedly a work song, setting the rhythmic beat and pace for oarsmen in the African tradition. It shows the sometimes blurred line between spirituals and other kinds of songs created by African-American slaves.*

Michael, row the boat ashore,
Hallelujah!
Michael's boat's a gospel boat,
Hallelujah!
I wonder where my mother's there,
Hallelujah!
See my mother on the rock going home,
Hallelujah!
On the rock going home in Jesus' name,
Hallelujah!
Michael's boat's a music boat,
Hallelujah!
Gabriel blows the trumpet horn,
Hallelujah!
O, you mind your boasting talk,
Hallelujah!
Boasting talk will sink your soul,
Hallelujah!
Brother, lend a helping hand,
Hallelujah!
Jordan's stream is wide and deep,
Hallelujah!
Jesus stand on the other side,
Hallelujah!

I wonder if my master's there,
Hallelujah!
My father's gone to an unknown land,
Hallelujah!
O, the Lord plants His garden there,
Hallelujah!
He raises the fruit for you to eat,
Hallelujah!
He that eats shall never die,
Hallelujah!
When the river overflows,
Hallelujah!
O, poor sinner, how's your land?
The river runs and darkness is coming,
Hallelujah!
Sinner, row to save your soul.
Michael, haul the boat ashore,
Then you'll hear the horn they blow,
Then you'll hear the trumpet sound,
Trumpet sound the world around;
Trumpet sound for rich and poor,
Trumpet sound the jubilee,
Trumpet sound for you and me.

O, Lord, These Bones of Mine

THE GREAT JAZZ MUSICIAN CHARLIE PARKER ONCE SAID, "MUSIC IS *your own experience, your thoughts, your wisdom. If you don't live it, it won't come out of your horn." That the African-American slaves lived their music is clear in these lyrics, which express the personal remaking that comes from sincere religious experience.*

O, Lord, these bones of mine,
O, Lord, these bones of mine,
O, Lord, these bones of mine,
Comin' together in the mornin'.

Some join the church to sing and shout,
Comin' together in the mornin',
Before six months they all turned out,
Comin' together in the mornin'.

I look at my hand and my hand look new,
Comin' together in the mornin',
I look at my foot and it look so too,
Comin' together in the mornin'.

The Old Ark's Moving, and I'm Going Home

UNCHARACTERISTIC OF SPIRITUALS AS A GENRE, "THE OLD ARK'S *Moving*" *has a decidedly light tone and even humorous lines. In fact, it resembles a blues song more than a hymn. This is not a "sorrow song," as W. E. B. Du Bois called the spirituals, but it is, in his words, "a gift of story and song . . . in an ill-harmonized and unmelodious land."*

O, the old ark's moving, moving, moving,
The old ark's moving
And I'm going home.

See that sister all dressed so fine?
She ain't got Jesus on her mind.
See that brother dressed so gay?
O, death's going to come carry him away.

See that sister there coming so slow?
She wants to get the Heaven before the
    Heaven door closes.
'Tain't but one thing on my mind.
My sister's gone to Heaven and left me
    behind.

O, the old ark's moving, moving, moving,
The old ark's moving,
And I'm going home.

The old ark she rocked,
The old ark she landed on the mountaintop.

O, the old ark's moving, moving, moving,
The old ark's moving,
And I'm going home.

The Old Sheep Know the Road

THIS SPIRITUAL BEGINS WITH A FOLK SAYING, MOVES TO AN ADMONI-tion to an errant brother, and then celebrates the spiritual freedom of the redeemed. Within its verses there are clues about the thoughts of those in bondage. Following the Civil War, most African Americans wanted to forget the spirituals, identifying them with a past they were eager to forget, transcend, and move beyond.

O, the old sheep know the road,
The old sheep know the road,
The old sheep know the road,
The young lambs must find the way.

O, sooner in the morning when I rise,
With crosses and trails on every side;
My brother, ain't you got your accounts all
    sealed?
You'd better go get them before you leave
    this field.

O, shout my sister, for you are free,
For Christ has bought you liberty;
I really do believe without one doubt,
That the Christian has a mighty right to
    shout.

My brother, better mind how you walk on
    the cross,
For your foot might slip and your soul get
    lost;
Better mind that sun and see how she runs,
And mind, don't let her catch you with your
    work undone.

O, the old sheep know the road,
The old sheep know the road,
The old sheep know the road,
The young lambs must find the way.

We'll Stand the Storm

Scholar and critic Harold Courlander writes that the spirituals express faith and hope in *"moving, immediate, colloquial, and often magnificently dramatic terms."* *"We'll Stand the Storm"* exemplifies those characteristics and serves as a testimony to the slaves' remarkable courage and steadfastness. There is a moving and profound spirit of hope in the words *"it won't be long."*

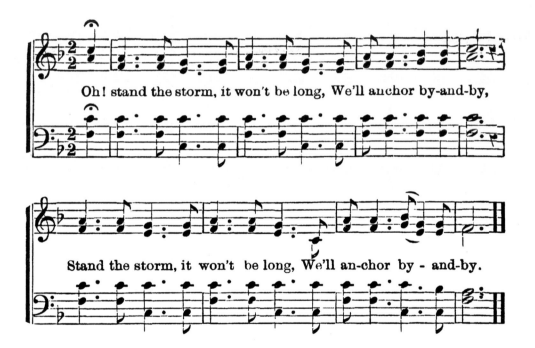

Oh! stand the storm, it won't be long, We'll anchor by-and-by,

Stand the storm, it won't be long, We'll an-chor by - and-by.

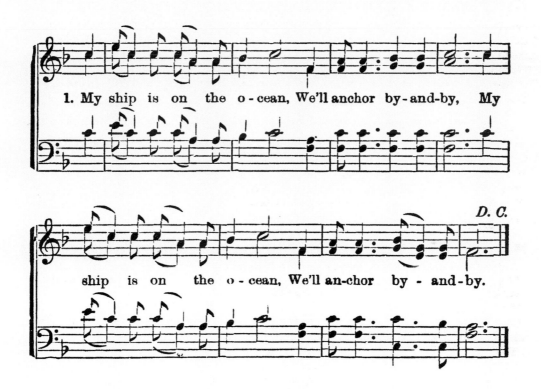

She's making for the kingdom,
We'll anchor . . .

I've a mother in the Kingdom,
We'll anchor . . .

Old Zion's Children Marching Along

THE UNIVERSALISM AND INTERNATIONAL APPEAL OF THE SPIRITUALS IS *reflected in a late nineteenth-century review from* Vienne der Tag, *an Austrian newspaper:* "And now that the Negro singers from the renowned Hampton Institute proceed in triumph through European concert halls they are not looked upon as foreigners but as interpreters of human experience common to mankind." *Worldwide, oppressed people are* "marching along / Talking about the welcome day."

Old Zion's children marching along,
Marching along, marching along;
Old Zion's children marching along,
Marching along, marching along,
Talking about the welcome day.

I hailed my mother in the morning,
Marching along, marching along,
Talking about the welcome day.

I hailed my brother in the morning,
Marching along, marching along,
Talking about the welcome day.

O, don't you want to live up yonder,
O, don't you want to live up yonder,
Talking about the welcome day.

Prayer Is the Key of Heaven

JAMES WELDON JOHNSON, WHO PUBLISHED HIS OWN SERMON POEMS IN God's Trombones, *also compiled spirituals. He wrote, "In the use of the English language both the bards and the group worked under limitations that might appear to be hopeless. . . . And yet there is poetry, and a surprising deal of it in the spirituals." What Johnson described as the "austerity" of white religion is transformed into something immediate and direct in lines like "Faith unlocks the door; / I know that."*

Prayer is the key of Heaven,
Prayer is the key of Heaven,
Prayer is the key of Heaven,
Faith unlocks the door;
I know that.

I think it was about twelve o'clock,
When Jesus led me to the rock;
I remember the day, I know the time,

Jesus freed this soul of mine;
My head got wet with the midnight dew,
The morning star was witness too.

Prayer is the key to Heaven,
Prayer is the key to Heaven,
Prayer is the key to Heaven,
Faith unlocks the door;
I know that.

Scandalize My Name

To "scandalize" a person's name means to bring discredit or dishonor to someone's reputation. *No one is safe from backbiting; one's own mother may be the perpetrator of damage. Despite the seriousness of being talked about, this spiritual also has a humorous side.*

I met my mother the other day,
I gave her my right hand,
An' just as soon as ever my back was turned,
She scandalize my name,
Scandalize my name,
Scandalize my name,
No, no. Scandalize my name.

I met my brother the other day;
I met my deacon the other day;
I met my elder the other day,
I gave him my right hand,
An' just as soon as ever my back was turned,
He scandalize my name,
Scandalize my name,
Scandalize my name,
No, no. Scandalize my name.

Sun Don't Set in the Morning

In this spiritual, a folk saying is set into a larger framework, a *context that radiates with hope. However insufferable their situation, the slaves knew: "Sun don't set in the morning / Light shines 'round the world."*

Sun don't set in the morning,
Sun don't set in the morning, Lord,
Sun don't set in the morning,
Light shines 'round the world.

Pray on, praying sister,
Pray on, praying sister,
Pray on, praying sister,
Light shines 'round the world.

Pray on, praying brother,
Pray on, praying brother,
Pray on, praying brother,
Light shines 'round the world.

Sun don't set in the morning,
Sun don't set in the morning, Lord,
Sun don't set in the morning,
Light shines 'round the world.

Sometimes I Feel Like a Motherless Child

THAT THE BLUES ARE SECULAR DESCENDANTS OF THE SPIRITUALS CAN BE *seen in one of their basic characteristics. Beneath the surface sadness, melancholy, and even despondency of blues lyrics, there is another reality: the wisdom of survivors who perceive the irony of their situation and are saved by this perception. As the novelist Ralph Ellison noted, they squeeze from it a "near-tragic, near-comic lyricism." And in this way they transcend their victimization to survive—and even prevail. Surely no loneliness surpasses that of "a motherless child / A long way from home," yet the very articulation of this state is a sign of endurance, dignity, and even hope.*

Sometimes I feel like a motherless child,
Sometimes I feel like a motherless child,
Sometimes I feel like a motherless child,
A long way from home,
A long way from home;
True believer;
A long way from home.

If this was judgment day,
If this was judgment day,
If this was judgment day,
Every little soul would pray,
Every little soul would pray;
True believer;
Every little soul would pray,

Sometimes I feel like I'm almost gone,
Sometimes I feel like I'm almost gone,
Sometimes I feel like I'm almost gone,
Way up in the heavenly land!
Way up in the heavenly land;
True believer;
Way up in the heavenly land!

Tell It

THE SLAVES SAW THE BIBLE AS AN ORGANIC WHOLE AND FOUND NO *inconsistency in including Abraham, David, Mary, and Paul in the same song. Also, they understood biblical characters as ancestors in the African tradition and assumed that at death all their spirits would be reunited at home in Africa.*

Father Abraham sitting down side-a the
  holy Lamb,
Way up on the mountaintop,
Tell it, tell it, tell it.
My Lord spoke and the chariot stop,
Sitting down side-a the holy Lamb.
Father Abraham sitting down side-a the
  holy Lamb.

Good-bye and fare you well,
Meet me around the throne of God;
Weep like a willow and mourn like a dove,
If you want to go to Heaven, you got to go
  by love.

M for Michael, G for Goliath,
D for little David done kill Goliath,
M for Mary, P for Paul,
C for Christ, He die for us all.

When I get to Heaven going to sit and tell
The three archangels to ring the bell;
When I get to Heaven going to sit and
  choose,
Going to ask my Lord for the silver shoes;
Sitting down side-a the holy Lamb,
Jeremiah sitting down side-a the holy Lamb.

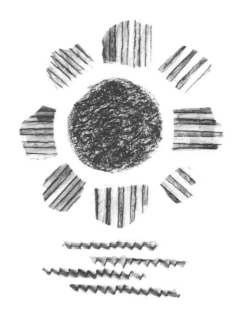

Were You There?

"WERE YOU THERE WHEN THEY CRUCIFIED MY LORD?" IS ONE OF THE most piercing and penetrating of the spirituals. It has all the direct and affecting impact of a Romare Bearden painting. The song's power lies in the way it confronts the hearer with the question of his or her immediate presence at Jesus' crucifixion. The list of details serves to heighten the dramatic involvement.

Were you there when they crucified my
  Lord?
Were you there?
Were you there when they crucified my
  Lord?
Were you there?
O, sometimes it causes me to tremble,
  tremble.

Were you there when they nailed Him to the
  tree?
To the tree?
Were you there when they nailed Him to the
  tree?
To the tree?
O, sometimes it causes me to tremble,
  tremble.

Were you there when they pierced Him in
  the side?
In the side?
Were you there when they pierced Him in
  the side?
O, sometimes it causes me to tremble,
  tremble.

Were you there when the sun refused to
  shine?
Refused to shine.
Were you there when the sun refused to
  shine?
Refused to shine.
O, sometimes it causes me to tremble,
  tremble.

Were you there when they laid Him in the
  tomb?
In the tomb?
Were you there when they laid Him in the
  tomb?
In the tomb?
O, sometimes it causes me to tremble,
  tremble.
Were you there when they laid Him in the
  tomb?

Wrestle On, Jacob

THIS SPIRITUAL CONTAINS SEVERAL BIBLICAL IMAGES FROM BOTH THE *Hebrew Bible and the New Testament. The story of Jacob's wrestling all night with the angel, however, is a persistently haunting one, and its full meaning can be as elusive as the stranger who would not tell Jacob his name. One view is that we are inextricably connected with those with whom we strive. In the spiritual's poetic words: "I hold my brother with a trembling hand," just as Jacob would not let the angel go.*

I hold my brother with a trembling hand,
The Lord will bless my soul,
Wrestle on, Jacob, Jacob,
Day is a-breaking,
Wrestle on, Jacob,
O, he would not let him go.

I will not let you go, my Lord,
Fisherman Peter out at sea.
He cast all night and he cast all day,

He catch no fish but he catch some soul;
Jacob hang from a trembling limb,
I looked to the east at the breaking of the
      day,
The old ship of Zion went sailing away.

Wrestle on, Jacob, Jacob,
Day is a-breaking,
Wrestle on, Jacob,
O, he would not let him go.

What You Going to Name That Pretty Little Baby?

IN THE SLAVE SYSTEM, A MOTHER AND CHILD COULD BE SEPARATED FROM *each other at any time by their owner, an act more cruel than physical torture and abuse. Naming a baby, therefore, was an occasion of courage as well as hope.*

O, Mary, what you going to name
That pretty little baby?
O, Mary, what you going to name
That pretty little baby?
Glory, glory, glory.

O, Mary, what you going to name
That pretty little baby?
O, Mary, what you going to name
That pretty little baby?
Glory, glory, glory.

Wrestling Jacob

JAMES WELDON JOHNSON, THE AFRICAN-AMERICAN ACTIVIST AND A *poet of note himself, called the unknown author of "Wrestling Jacob" a "lyrical genius." The words are based on the biblical story of Jacob, although the music historian Maud Cuney Hare says there is a similar story among the Bula people of the Cameroons, and she suggests that many spirituals are based on African tales. In the biblical account in Genesis, Jacob wrestles with a stranger, who finally blesses him and changes his name to Israel "for you have struggled with God and with men and you have won."*

1. Wrest-ling Ja-cob, Ja-cob, day is a-breaking,

Wrest-ling Ja-cob, Ja-cob, I will not let thee go.

Let me go, Ja-cob. I will not let thee go.

Wrest-ling Ja - cob, Ja - cob, I will not let thee go. I'll
(Or this.) I'll

hold thee till the break of day, I will not let thee go, Un -
wres - tle till the break of day, I will not let thee go, Un -

til thou tell me what's thy name, I will not let thee go.
til thou come and bless my soul, I will not let thee go.

Trouble Done Bore Me Down

The whole genre of spirituals has a special poignancy because of the extraordinary circumstances under which they were composed: 250 years of chattel slavery. The sheer totality of the slave system must inevitably have led to "troubles" that literally pressed men and women to the ground in despair. But as singer-activist Paul Robeson writes, there is "healing comfort to be found in the illimitable sorrow of the spirituals." Singing the spirituals lifted the slaves beyond the pain of oppression by providing hope for a day of liberation.

O Lord, O Lord,
What shall I do?
Trouble done bore me down.
O Lord, O Lord,
What shall I do?
O, trouble done bore me down.

He's gone on high to prepare a place,
Trouble done bore me down;
For to prepare a place for me and you,
Trouble done bore me down.

O Lord, O Lord,
Have mercy on me,
Trouble done bore me down;
O Lord, O Lord,
Have mercy on me,
O, trouble done bore me down.

I've seen some strangers quite unknown,
Trouble done bore me down;
I'm a child of misery,
Trouble done bore me down.

I'm sometimes up and sometimes down;
Trouble done bore me down;
I'm sometimes level with the ground,
Trouble done bore me down.

O Lord, O Lord,
What shall I do?
Trouble done bore me down.
O Lord, O Lord,
What shall I do?
O, trouble done bore me down.

I bent my knees and smote the ground,
Trouble done bore me down;
I asked God almighty for to run me 'round.
Trouble done bore me down.

O Lord, O Lord,
What shall I do?
Trouble done bore me down.
O Lord, O Lord,
What shall I do?
O, trouble done bore me down.

When I was a moaner just like you,
Trouble done bore me down;
I moaned till the Lord God set me free,
Trouble done bore me down.

O Lord, O Lord,
Take pity on me,
Trouble done bore me down;
O Lord, O Lord,
Take pity on me,
O, trouble done bore me down.

This bed of sin on which I lie,
Trouble done bore me down;
I lay my body down to die,
Trouble done bore me down.

O Lord, O Lord,
Take pity on me,
Trouble done bore me down;
O Lord, O Lord,
Take pity on me,
O, trouble done bore me down.

Good-bye

IT IS FITTING TO CONCLUDE WITH A SPIRITUAL THAT WAS SUNG AT THE *end of a religious meeting. This song, collected in Charleston, South Carolina, was included in the first anthology of spirituals,* Slave Songs of the United States, *published in 1867. A typical slave service would break up with everyone singing this song while shaking hands with everyone else, and incorporating into the lyrics the name of the person whose hand was being shaken.*

Good-bye, my brother, good-bye,
  Hallelujah!
Good-bye, Sister Sally, good-bye,
  Hallelujah!

Going home, Hallelujah!
Jesus call me, Hallelujah!
Linger no longer, Hallelujah!
Tarry no longer, Hallelujah!

Further Reading

Allen, William Francis, Charles Pickard Ware, and Lucy McKim Garrison, eds. *Slave Songs of the United States*. New York: Dover Publications, 1955. Reprint of 1867 edition.

Carawan, Guy, and Candie Carawan. *Sing for Freedom: The Story of the Civil Rights Movement Through Its Songs*. Bethlehem, Pa.: Sing Out, 1990.

Cataliotti, Robert H. *The Music in African American Fiction*. New York: Garland Publishing, 1995.

Cone, James H. *The Spirituals and the Blues: An Interpretation*. New York: Seabury Press, 1972.

Du Bois, William E. B. *The Souls of Black Folk*. New York: Bantam Books, 1989. Reprint of 1903 edition.

Epstein, Dena J. *Sinful Tunes and Spirituals: Black Folk Music to the Civil War*. Urbana: University of Illinois Press, 1977.

Fisher, Miles Mark. *Negro Slave Songs of the United States*. New York: Citadel Press, 1990. Reprint of 1953 edition.

Hurston, Zora Neale. "Spirituals and Neo-Spirituals." In Nancy Cunard, ed., *Negro: Anthology Made by Nancy Cunard 1931–33*. London: Wishart & Co., 1934, 359–61.

Johnson, James Weldon, and J. Rosamond Johnson. *The Books of American Negro Spirituals, Including "The Book of American Negro Spirituals" and "The Second Book of Negro Spirituals."* New York: DaCapa Press, 1969. Reprint of 1925 and 1926 editions.

Levine, Lawrence W. "Slave Songs and Slave Consciousness: An Exploration in Neglected Sources." In Timothy E. Fulop and Albert J. Raboteau, eds., *African-American Religion: Interpretive Essays in Religion and Culture*. New York: Routledge, 1997, 57–87.

Lewis, Theophilus. "The Negro Spirituals as Hymns of a People." *America* 61 (22 April 1939): 43–44.

Lovell, John, Jr. *Black Song: The Forge and the Flame. The Story of How the Afro-American Spirit Was Hammered Out*. New York: Paragon House, 1986. Reprint of 1972 edition.

Marsh, J. B. T. *The Story of the Jubilee Singers; With Their Songs*. Rev. ed. Boston: Houghton, Osgood, 1880.

Newman, Richard. *Everybody Say Freedom: Everything You Need to Know about African-American History*. New York: Plume/Penguin, 1996.

Peters, Erskine, ed. *Lyrics of the Afro-American Spiritual: A Documentary Collection*. Westport, Conn.: Greenwood Press, 1993.

Raboteau, Albert J. *Slave Religion: The "Invisible Institution" in the Antebellum South*. New York: Oxford University Press, 1978.

Radano, Ronald. "The Writing of the Spirituals." *Critical Inquiry* 22 (Spring 1996): 506–44.

Southern, Eileen. *The Music of Black Americans: A History*. New York: W. W. Norton, 1971.

Spencer, Jon Michael. *Black Hymnody: A Hymnological History of the African-American Church*. Knoxville: University of Tennessee Press, 1992.

———. *Protest and Praise: Sacred Music of Black Religion*. Minneapolis: Fortress Press, 1990.

Thurman, Howard. *Deep Rivers and the Negro Spiritual Speaks of Life and Death*. Richmond, Ind.: Friends Press, 1990. Reprint of 1975 edition.

Work, John W., ed. *American Negro Songs and Spirituals*. New York: Bonanza Books, 1940.

Index